Healthcare of Young People:

promotion in primary care

D1387240

Ann McPherson

Chris Donovan

Aidan Macfarlane

Radcliffe Medical Press

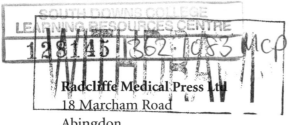

Radcliffe Medical Press Ltd
18 Marcham Road
Abingdon
Oxon OX14 1AA
United Kingdom

www.radcliffe-oxford.com
The Radcliffe Medical Press electronic catalogue and online ordering facility.
Direct sales to anywhere in the world.

© 2002 Ann McPherson, Chris Donovan and Aidan Macfarlane

British Library Cataloguing in Publication Data

A catalogue record for this book is available from the British Library.

ISBN 1 85775 498 0

Typeset by Advance Typesetting Ltd, Oxon.
Printed and bound by T J International Ltd, Padstow, Cornwall

Contents

About the authors

Ann McPherson CBE FRCGP FRCP DCH has been a GP in Oxford since 1979. She is also a part-time lecturer in the Department of General Practice, Oxford University and a Fellow of the Royal College of General Practitioners and of Green College, Oxford. She writes on, and researches into, the health of adolescents and women. She is co-author, with Aidan Macfarlane, of several books for teenagers and their parents, including *Diary of a Teenage Health Freak*, which is based on research in schools about teenage health related behaviours, as well as writing a website www.teenagehealthfreak.org. She is Chair of the Adolescent Working Party of the Royal College of General Practitioners and a member of the Independent Advisory Group on Teenage Pregnancy.

Aidan Macfarlane FRCP FRCPCH FFPHM set up and was Director of the National Adolescent and Student Health Unit as well as Commissioner of the Child and Adolescent Health Services for Oxfordshire Health Authority. He currently works as an international consultant in the strategic planning of child and adolescent health services. He is a member of the Adolescent Working Party of the Royal College of General Practitioners and of the Intercollegiate Working Party of the Royal College of Paediatrics and Child Health. He has published extensively on adolescent health in conjunction with Dr Ann McPherson, with whom he runs the above-mentioned website for teenagers www.teenagehealthfreak.org.

Chris Donovan MA (Oxon) MRCGP worked as a GP in North London for over 30 years. During those years he was a trainer, course organiser and part-time senior lecturer at The Royal Free Hospital. Ten years ago he founded and chaired the RCGP Adolescent Working Party, whose publications committee has produced several training manuals and trigger videos on adolescent health in general practice. When he left the practice he worked as a part-time consultant in the long term follow-up clinic for cancer patients at Great Ormond Street Hospital and was medical adviser at The Thomas Coram Foundation (now Coram Family). He is currently Vice Chair of the RCGP Adolescent Working Party, Chair of Brent Centre for Young People and an Honorary Senior Lecturer in the Centre for Community Child Health at The Royal Free Hospital Medical School.

Acknowledgements

We would like to express our enormous gratitude to all the members of the Adolescent Working Party of the Royal College of General Practitioners. This really is a joint effort by all those below, who have now worked together on developing adolescent health services in the UK for several years. This manual represents an edited version of all their work.

Professor Ruth Chambers

Dr John Coleman

Dr Dick Churchill

Dr Marian Davis

Dr Chris Donovan

Professor Elena Garralda

Dr Lionel Jacobson

Dr Caroline Mawer

Ms Judy McRae

Ms Sara Richards

Dr Hilary Smith

Dr Richard Burack

We would particularly like to thank Alison Hadley and Catherine Dennison from the Teenage Pregnancy Unit, and all the staff at the Trust for the Study of Adolescence, for the enormous amount of research and work that they carried out on our behalf. Thanks to Janet Bell, Practice Manager at the Maltings Surgery, Hertfordshire, for the provision of several of the case studies in Chapter 6. Thanks are due also to the Child Growth Foundation for their permission to reproduce the percentile charts in the Appendix and to Harlow Printing for supplying these charts.

The protocol and guidelines for issuing emergency contraception for young people in primary care is adapted from guidelines provided by Dr Liz Greenhall and colleagues at the Alex Turnbull Clinic, Oxford.

Much of the 'data' in Chapter 4 comes from *Key Data on Adolescence 2001* by J Coleman and J Schofield, published by the Trust for the Study of Adolescence. We are indebted to the many researchers who produced the original data.

Chapter 1

Introduction to this manual

Adolescents have health needs which have to be met by the primary healthcare team just as patients of any other age group do, but they also have specific needs relative to their age. The purpose of this manual is to provide essential, pragmatic and useful information for primary healthcare professionals in order to help them meet these needs.

This manual follows on from *The Health of Adolescents in Primary Care: how to promote adolescent health in your practice* and it is designed for general practitioners, practice managers, practice receptionists and other members of the primary healthcare team. It is not necessary to be an expert in adolescent health to use it!

The reasons for highlighting the needs of adolescents are that:

- many health related behaviours such as smoking, diet, alcohol use and sexuality begin during this period and can have profound implications on their health as they continue into adulthood

- disadvantaged adolescents are more likely to develop lifestyles that put their health at risk and primary healthcare can help compensate for this

- although most adolescents consider themselves to be healthy, 21% of male adolescents and 16% of female adolescents class themselves as having a longstanding illness

- there are a number of independent sources of information about teenage health matters available, to which the primary healthcare team can now refer adolescents, including websites such as www.teenagehealthfreak.org

- young people are not used to using health services such as primary healthcare and therefore need encouragement to use these services appropriately and need to be assured about the confidential nature of the services

- there is now excellent information available to primary healthcare members about training in adolescent health on the Internet at www.euteach.com. (EuTEACH = European Training in Effective Adolescent Care and Health).

How to use this manual

This manual is designed to be useful to all members of the primary healthcare team. It is most useful to look first at how 'user friendly' your practice is at present, and you can then look at the '10 tips' on how to make your practice more user friendly. The rest of the manual is designed to support this aim and you can photocopy, reproduce and use any part of the manual that you wish without applying for copyright, excluding the percentile charts in the Appendix.

If you have any suggestions as to how the manual can be improved, please contact one of the authors.

Chapter 2

How does your practice rate with teenagers?

Checklist

1 Do you have a written practice confidentiality policy for young people aged 16 and under?

   Yes   No

2 Do you see under 16-year-olds without a parent?

   Yes   No

3 Do you have a notice in your waiting room about 'emergency contraception'?

   Yes   No

4 Do you have magazines and leaflets in your waiting room specifically for young people?

   Yes   No

5 Do you have a practice information leaflet specifically for teenagers or are teenagers mentioned in your practice pamphlet?

   Yes   No

6 Have you ever had a practice meeting to discuss the needs of young people?

Yes   No

7 Have all members of the practice had training in how to deal with young people?

Yes   No

8 Do you provide contraception to young people aged under 16?

Yes   No

9 Do you run clinics specifically for young people?

Yes   No

10 Does your practice provide teenagers with free condoms?

Yes   No

Score

1 to 5 – should be able to do much better

6 to 8 – still room for improvement

9 to 10 – teenagers will be flocking to your practice.

Chapter 3

Getting it right for teenagers in your practice – 10 tips

1 **Organise a whole team practice meeting to look at ways in which to improve the 'teenage friendliness' of the practice.**
Everybody needs to be aboard – the GPs, the practice nurses, the health visitors, the secretaries, the receptionists. When young people are asked what they want from their practice, apart from confidentiality, friendliness rates as the highest. A team meeting specifically on the subject of how to ensure that the practice is friendly to young people gives all the team members new ideas. Do a quick audit to see what you are offering – not what you *think* you are offering!
   Things to look at are as follows.

   - Are there posters and literature in the waiting room (or toilets) directed at young people?

   - Are there leaflets for young people that are user friendly (at least 50% pictures and glossy) and that use appropriate language?

   - Get each member of the team to imagine that they are a teenager coming into the surgery with a problem or wanting contraception and tell the rest of the team how you think they would feel.

2 **Identify the characteristics of the 10–18-year-olds in your practice.** Using the practice's 'age/sex' register, along with a degree of common sense, it should be relatively easy to work out a profile for this age group. Only then can you start to identify their needs.

- Total number in practice.

- Percentage of these seen in the last year.

- Number asking for contraceptive advice.

- Gender breakdown.

- Information on smoking and alcohol.

3 **Train appropriate practice members in contraception, including emergency contraception (EC).** GPs, nurses and receptionists all need to be trained on their interaction with teenagers coming in for contraception. Be sensitive to their embarrassment – they won't give you a second chance to get it right. Contraception and preventing teenage pregnancy cannot be seen in isolation from all the other services provided by the practice for this age group.

- Advertise in large letters in the waiting room that emergency contraception is available.

- Make sure that the receptionists do not ask embarrassing 'whys' about emergency appointments.

- If a practice doctor is unwilling to give emergency contraception make sure that alternative sources are available and that the young people are directed towards these without being made to feel guilty.

4 **Inform young people as to what the practice provides.**

- Have posters showing what services the practice provides for young people, so that when they come in for something else they know that they can get contraceptive advice.

- Develop a special 'Practice Information' booklet for teenagers, which covers all the practice services including contraception, sports injuries, counselling, emergency contraception, abortion, eating disorders, etc. Provide for all the young people identified by the 'age/sex' register.

- Write a 'birthday letter' to all young people when they become 16 (or earlier), explaining about the practice and pointing out that when they reach 16 they can register with their choice of GP should they wish to do so and get contraceptive advice from any GP willing to offer the service.

- Make sure they know how to register as a temporary patient.

5 **Make confidentiality a priority practice issue.** Adolescents are aware of the fact that much of what they say about themselves and the way in which they behave is not treated as confidential by their family, friends, peers and teachers. Contact with the primary healthcare team may be the first time that the concept of confidentiality will be raised with them. It is essential that the practice puts out a positive message about confidentiality.

- By using posters, e.g. Brook poster 'Hear to listen not to tell' (*see* Chapter 19, page 123 for details of Brook Advisory Service).

- Get supplies of the leaflet 'Private and Confidential – Talking to Doctors' – available from Brook Advisory Service.

- Reassure young people about confidentiality during face-to-face consultations.

- Make sure that every member of the practice is signed up to a 'confidentiality code of practice' and is aware of the *Confidentiality Toolkit* (*see* Chapter 19, page 111).

6 **Advertise services that are available for young people outside of the practice.** The practice services are only one source of help. Young people need to know what other sources are available, including:

- young people's clinics, including Brook Advisory Service

- family planning clinics
- other GPs
- Accident and Emergency departments
- condom machines in toilets.

7 **Consider organising a young person's clinic.** These work in some practices and not in others. It is usually dependent on the personality of the person running the clinic, the characteristics of the local teenage population, other GP practices joining in, etc. Note the following points.

- It takes time not only for teenagers to find out about the clinics, but also to build up confidence in them.
- Try running them at times convenient for teenagers, i.e. immediately after school.
- Try doing them in conjunction with the school nurse within the school setting.
- Make the environment very teenage-friendly by asking the advice of the teenagers themselves.

8 **Involve parents.** During the teenage years parents still continue to be the main providers, carers, and sources of health information to teenagers. This needs to be supported and respected.

- Provide information for parents about the practice facilities available for teenagers and other resources including information on depression, drugs, eating disorders, etc.
- Make sure that parents know how to provide information about contraception in general and emergency contraception in particular.
- Discuss with young people the advantages of involving their parents in their sexually related decisions.

9 **Offer advice and support for teenagers who do get pregnant.**
If a teenager does get pregnant, make sure that they are given
support and help in coming to a decision as to whether to
continue with the pregnancy or to have a termination, without
indulging in moral attitudes.

- If they want to continue with the pregnancy, try to get them
  to involve their parents and put them in contact with
  supporting agencies including the health visitor.

- If they decide to have a termination arrange for a rapid
  referral.

- If you are opposed to termination (for any reason) make
  sure that the young person is not made to feel guilty and get
  them to see another doctor immediately.

10 **Make sure that the practice advice is directed to young men
as well as young women.** Remember young men. Let them
know they are welcome too. When advertising contraceptive
services direct the information to males and females even if the
practice only gets 'paid' for services to young women. Aim to
include:

- free condoms

- advice about emergency contraception and STIs

- posters in waiting room aimed directly at young men.

Chapter 4

Facts and figures

Useful national background facts and figures about adolescents and their health

Children and adolescents aged 0–19 years make up a quarter of the UK population.

- There are 3.6 million 10–14-year-olds in the UK.
- There are 3.4 million 15–19-year-olds in the UK.

Consultation with GPs

- Approximately a quarter of all young people of both genders have seen their GP in the last three months.
- 7% of boys and 11% of girls aged 13–15 have seen their GP in the previous two weeks.
- 6% of boys and 10% of girls aged 16–17 have seen their GP in the previous two weeks.
- 9% of boys and 21% of girls aged 18–20 have seen their GP in the previous two weeks.
- Over 52% of young people prefer seeing their doctor alone, 39% want to go with a friend and 27% want to go with a parent.

- The average consultation time that a teenager has with their GP is approximately two minutes shorter than for adults (6 minutes versus 8 minutes).

Main causes of death amongst 15–19-year-olds in the UK 1994–96, by gender

- In boys, 42% of deaths were due to accidents, 14% due to suicide, 8% due to neoplasms (of which 3% are due to leukaemia), 7% disorders of the nervous system and 5% due to mental disorders.
- In girls, 29% of deaths were due to accidents, 10% due to suicide, 18% due to neoplasms (of which 5% are due to leukaemia), 7% disorders of the nervous system and 3% due to mental disorders.

Conception rates for women under 20 in 1999

- For women aged 13–15 the conception rate is 8.9 per 1000, of which 53% are terminated.
- For women aged 15–19 the conception rate is 64 per 1000, of which 38% are terminated.

Where do adolescents go for advice on specific conditions?

- For spots and acne – 51% would go to their GP, 39% to nobody, 1% to the school nurse, 5% to a clinic and 4% to 'other'.
- For advice about their diet – 30% would go to their GP, 50% to nobody, 9% to the school nurse, 4% to a clinic and 7% to 'other'.
- For advice about smoking – 16% would go to their GP, 64% to nobody, 9% to the school nurse, 3% to a clinic and 8% to 'other'.
- For advice about pregnancy – 26% would go to their GP, 34% to nobody, 4% to the school nurse, 30% to a clinic and 5% to 'other'.

- For advice about STIs – 18% would go to their GP, 58% to nobody, 9% to the school nurse, 8% to a clinic and 6% to 'other'.

Main sources of information about sex

- For 12–13-year-old boys, 35% got information from school lessons, 21% from parents, 18% from friends, 14% from TV and films, 3% from magazines, 1% from the school nurse.

- For 14–15-year-old boys, 27% got information from school lessons, 15% from parents, 29% from friends, 17% from TV and films, 4% from magazines, 1% from the school nurse.

- For 12–13-year-old girls, 26% got information from school lessons, 30% from parents, 19% from friends, 4% from TV and films, 11% from magazines, 2% from the school nurse.

- For 14–15-year-old girls, 18% got information from school lessons, 19% from parents, 28% from friends, 3% from TV and films, 21% from magazines, less than 1% from the school nurse.

Contraceptive services

Used by girls during the five years prior to interview, by age.

- For 16–17-year-old girls, 25% had visited their own GP, 17% a family planning clinic, 2% another GP, 62% had not visited anywhere.

- For 18–19-year-old girls, 57% had visited their own GP, 18% a family planning clinic, 1% another GP, 31% had not visited anywhere.

Knowledge of contraceptive services available in their area.

- 7% of boys aged 12–13 knew of any local contraceptive services.

- 25% of boys aged 14–15 knew of any local contraceptive services.

- 12% of girls aged 12–13 knew of any local contraceptive services.
- 46% of girls aged 14–15 knew of any local contraceptive services.

Regular use of condoms amongst 16–19-year-olds, by gender.

- For young men having sex, 68% always used them, 18% usually used them, and 13% sometimes used them.
- For young women having sex, their partners always used them 57% of times, usually used them 17% of times, sometimes used them 26% of times.

Attitudes to provision of primary healthcare services amongst young people

- 80% rated confidentiality as important, 50% rated having a doctor interested in teenage problems important, 39% rated seeing a doctor the same day as making the appointment as important, 39% rated having a special drop-in teenage clinic as important, 33% wanted to be able to choose the sex of their doctor, 32% wanted to be able to ask advice over the 'phone without having to give their name, 30% felt that friendly receptionists were important.
- Amongst teenagers who had difficulties with their GP consultation – 40% of males and 44% of females gave the reason as 'difficulty in getting a quick appointment', 46% of males and 63% of females found it 'embarrassing to talk about personal concerns', 21% of males and 32% of females 'found the doctor unsympathetic', 25% of males and 32% of females were 'concerned their parents would find out'.

UK prevalence of psychiatric disorders amongst 16–19-year-olds, by gender

Table 4.1: Rates per 1000 population

	Males	Females
Alcohol dependence	113	68
Drug dependence	79	56
Mixed anxiety and depressive disorders	33	87
Panic disorder	14	4
Depressive episode	8	32
Generalised anxiety disorder	6	4
All phobias	4	45
Obsessive-compulsive disorder	3	12
Functional psychoses	3	–

Experience of being bullied at school amongst 11–15-year-olds, by gender

- 51% of boys and 47% of girls had never been bullied.

- 23% of boys and 31% of girls had been bullied in the past, though not in the school term that the questionnaire was given out.

- 13% of boys and girls had been bullied once or twice during the term.

- 3% of boys and 2% of girls were bullied several times a week.

Medication taken by young people over the previous week

Table 4.2: Percentages

	12–13 years		14–15 years	
	Male	Female	Male	Female
Asthma	13.4	12.4	10.5	12.7
Colds, throat or flu	22.7	32.4	23.9	34.4
Diabetes	1.1	0.8	0.8	0.8
Eczema	4.9	8.0	4.1	8.6
Other skin problems	6.7	10.3	9.3	14.4
Epilepsy	0.8	0.7	0.6	0.4
Hay fever or allergies	7.3	8.9	8.3	11.2
None of these	60.4	49.7	59.0	44.7

Young people and dieting

- Of boys aged 13–16, 5% were dieting to lose weight, 17% felt they should be dieting to lose weight and 78% were happy with their weight.

- Of girls aged 13–16, 15% were dieting to lose weight, 27% felt they should be dieting to lose weight, and 58% were happy with their weight.

Sports and physical activity

- 23% of girls and 12% of boys had got out of breath playing sport once a week.

- 5% of girls and 3% of boys had never got out of breath playing sport.

- 30% of girls and 25% of boys had got out of breath playing sport 2–3 times a week.

- 15% of girls and 29% of boys had got out of breath playing sport every day.

- Outside of school and on a weekly basis, soccer was played by 63% of boys and 10% of girls, swimming was undertaken by 21% of boys and 25% of girls, riding a bicycle was undertaken by 53% of boys and 29% of girls, no sport was done by 5% of boys and 14% of girls.

Hours per day spent watching television amongst secondary school age young people, by gender

- 1% of boys and girls watch no television every day.
- 22% of boys and girls watched 30–60 minutes of television every day.
- 27% of boys and girls watched more than 4 hours of television every day.

Smoking by the age of 16

- One third of young people will never have smoked a cigarette.
- One third will have tried smoking but given up.
- One third will be smoking on a regular basis.

Illegal drugs

By the age of 15:

- 61% of boys and girls have been offered illegal drugs.
- 38% of boys and 33% of girls have tried illegal drugs.
- 31% of boys and 30% of girls have tried cannabis.
- 8% of boys and girls are regular cannabis users.
- Of all young people trying illegal drugs, 96% experiment with them and 4% abuse them.

Alcohol

At the age of 15:

- The mean alcohol intake in the previous seven days was 5 units for boys and 3 units for girls.
- Of those drinking alcohol, 37% of boys and 18% of girls had drunk beer in the last seven days.
- Of those drinking alcohol, 18% of boys and 25% of girls had drunk wine in the last seven days.
- Of those drinking alcohol, 17% of boys and girls had drunk spirits.

Sex

Wellings K *et al.* (2001) Sexual behaviour in Britain: early hetero-sexual experience. *The Lancet.* **358:** 1843–50.

Sample 11 161 men and women.

- The proportion of those aged 16–19 years reporting first heterosexual intercourse at younger than 16 years was 30% of men and 26% of women.
- The proportion of women reporting first intercourse before 16 years of age increased up to, but not after, the 1990s.
- There has been a sustained increase in condom use and a decline of men and women reporting no contraceptive use at first intercourse, with decreasing age.
- Early age of first intercourse was significantly associated with pregnancy under 18 years but not with the occurrence of STIs.
- Low educational attainment was associated with motherhood before 18 years but not with abortion.

Chapter 5

Confidentiality and consent

Introduction

Confidentiality about the health consultation is, for young people, their single greatest concern. It is therefore essential, in order to win the confidence of young people, that your practice gets this aspect of their care right. Below are some key points to help you do this, but for greater detail in order to help you to implement a practice policy on 'confidentiality and consent' please use the *Confidentiality Toolkit* which is available from the Royal College of General Practitioners (*see* Chapter 19, page 111).

Key points

- 'Consent' means that the young person agrees to the examination or treatment being proposed.
- 'Confidentiality' means that the professional has a duty not to disclose anything learned during a consultation, without that person's agreement.
- Every practice should have its own confidentiality policy which includes 'confidentiality and young people' – this needs to be

advertised to young people in the practice leaflet and on a waiting room poster.

- Improving young people's trust in the confidentiality of the practice will help remove one of the main obstacles that deters some teenagers from seeking help.
- All members of the practice should sign up to the practice confidentiality policy.
- Confidentiality can be broken in only the most exceptional circumstances, when the health, safety or welfare of the patient or others would otherwise be at grave risk.
- The decision to break confidentiality depends on the degree of current or potential risk, not on the age of the patient.
- A young person is said to be 'competent' to consent if the health professional believes he or she is capable of understanding the choices of treatment available and their consequences.
- Young people worry about deliberate breaches of confidentiality to parents, especially concerning pregnancy; informal inadvertent breaches during a parents' visit to the same practice; gossipy receptionists and confidential information sent by post and intercepted.
- If an accidental breach of information does occur then there needs to be protocol to follow, which includes a full apology and explanation to the young person concerned.

Legal issues

Details of legal issues are constantly changing and it is wise for your team to remain aware of how the courts are interpreting issues concerning 'consent', 'right to refusal', etc, on a year-to-year basis.

Confidentiality and consent concerning contraception and young people

---

A young person can be given contraception advice and contraception even if under 16 if …

- The young person understands the doctor's advice.

- The doctor cannot persuade the young person to inform his or her parents, or to allow the doctor to inform the parents, that he or she is seeking contraceptive advice.

- The young person is very likely to begin or continue having sexual intercourse with or without contraception.

- Unless he or she receives contraception the young person's physical and/or mental health are likely to suffer.

- The young person's best interests require the doctor to give contraceptive advice, treatment, or both, without parental consent.

These are the Fraser guidelines issued following a House of Lords judgement in 1985.

Problems in applying a confidentiality policy

Deciding if an adolescent is 'competent' is a subjective professional judgement. There are few accepted criteria. Where does an adolescent with Down's syndrome or a learning difficulty stand? At what age does a young person acquire competence? It is wise when dealing with borderline cases to discuss this with a colleague, a defence society or the Ethical Committee of the BMA. A record of the professional's reasoning should be made in the notes in case the judgement is questioned in court.

Refusal

To some the patient's power to refuse is the partner of the power to give consent.

This is not the way the courts have interpreted the House of Lords ruling. Even when the court accepts that the adolescent is competent, it can and often has overruled the young person's wishes, arguing that it is in their best interests. Examples include forcing treatment on anorexics, psychotics and Jehovah's witnesses.

Parental rights

Even though adolescents have the right to consent and to confidentiality, their parents in normal circumstances are their greatest source of support. Every effort should be made by the professional to persuade the patient to inform their parents or to allow the doctor to do so. However, there are no accepted guidelines indicating what is meant by 'every effort'. The professional is advised to discuss difficult cases with a colleague and record their reasoning in the notes.

Breaking confidentiality

This again raises the question, what is meant by '… the health, safety or welfare of the patient or others would otherwise be at grave risk'?

When borderline cases arise like being told of bullying in school, violence in the family, or a crime like pushing drugs, the team is advised to discuss and if necessary seek outside help.

Checklist – reviewing and developing confidentiality in your practice

1 Does your practice have a policy on confidentiality?
   ☐ Yes   ☐ No

2 Is this a written confidentiality policy?
   ☐ Yes   ☐ No

3 Does the policy mention teenagers and young people under 16?
   ☐ Yes   ☐ No

4 When was the confidentiality policy last discussed at a practice meeting?
   ☐ Less than 3 months ago   ☐ 3–12 months ago
   ☐ More than 1 year ago   ☐ Never

5 Do new members of the team have to sign up to the confidentiality policy when they join?
   ☐ Yes   ☐ No

6 Is there a statement about confidentiality and young people in your practice leaflet?
   ☐ Yes   ☐ No

7 Does it specifically mention young people under 16?
   ☐ Yes   ☐ No

8 Are there notices in your practice which explain the confidentiality policy …
   … in the waiting room/reception area?
   ☐ Yes   ☐ No
   … in the corridors?
   ☐ Yes   ☐ No

... in the GP consulting rooms?

☐ Yes   ☐ No

... in the nurse consulting rooms?

☐ Yes   ☐ No

9 Do members of your team meet to discuss issues in applying the confidentiality policy when they arise, for example at practice meetings?

☐ Yes   ☐ No

10 Do you provide training in how to apply your confidentiality policy for ...

... receptionists?

☐ Yes   ☐ No

... nurses?

☐ Yes   ☐ No

... GPs?

☐ Yes   ☐ No

... secretaries and other members of staff?

☐ Yes   ☐ No

Quotes from young people as to how they see 'confidentiality' in practice

What they believe confidentiality should be:

'Confidentiality at the doctors means he can't tell anyone what you say ... your mum, your family. No one.'

'It means you can trust your doctor – you can tell him anything.'

What it would mean in practice:

'You think he won't tell anyone. Well you hope *he won't.'*

'They're not supposed *to tell anyone.'*

'Of course they need your parents' consent for the Pill – sex under 16 is illegal. It's the law.'

'I thought it was only confidential if you're over 16, I thought they could notify your parents if you were younger.'

What they worry about with doctors:

'It's supposed to be confidential, but you wonder what they might be saying informally.'

'Doctors are sly … especially if they know your family, you don't know what they'd let slip.'

'You know that when your mum goes down the week after, something might slip out and it's just too scary.'

What they worry about with receptionists:

'Receptionists are only supposed to call up files in an emergency, or if a doctor asks them, but I reckon they have a snoop anyway. It's just human nature.'

'If they got found out they would get fired 'cos they're not supposed to tell anyone, but they tell when they're having a pint down the pub, well, it's not very professional is it?'

'She probably would tell your mum if she knew her well … out of worry … or just out of respect really.'

'She might say, "Oh Leanne was down here the other day. She was waiting a long time."'

Chapter 6

The consultation and case studies

Individual adolescent consultations

Communicating with teenagers requires all the skill used with any patient, i.e. putting them at their ease, active listening, building trust, using open-ended questions, providing time and giving clear explanations.

There are some aspects of consulting with this age group that can cause particular difficulties and members of the team might find it profitable to discuss them.

Acute embarrassment

Most adolescents are not used to seeing a GP or nurse on their own. They may find themselves consulting for the first time over an acutely embarrassing personal problem they cannot share with their family. Even young people who are used to seeing doctors and nurses because they have a chronic condition like diabetes or cancer, may find it embarrassing to discuss their personal problems or the physical development changes they are experiencing.

Because of this embarrassment it takes more time and can be difficult to put the youngster at their ease at the start of the consultation, in fact it may take more than one contact.

Parents

Embarrassment over personal problems can be increased when a parent is present. Around 60% of 15–16-year-olds consult with a parent in the room. Simple GP enquiries in these circumstances, e.g. about alcohol, sex or drugs are likely to elicit both inadequate and embarrassed answers. Asking parents to withdraw can also be tricky unless the GP or nurse is known to do this on a regular basis or has already discussed the reasons with the parents. For example, as explained, it is good to see teenagers on their own at the end of the consultation in order to build up a relationship and provide the young patient with a chance of gaining experience in consulting on their own.

When a parent is not present they can still cause concern for both the patient and the doctor. The main worry here is what the parents may hear about the interaction once it is over.

It is important that the doctor mentions the practice policy on confidentiality during sensitive consultations and agrees with the patient on what will be said to a parent should either be asked.

Most adolescents receive their main support from their families so openness needs to be encouraged, as long as it appears to be in the patient's best interests.

Time

It takes time to build up trust and to put a young patient at ease so that they feel they can speak freely. It has been shown that in some practices adolescent consultations are shorter than those with adults. Is this because adolescents bring simpler clinical problems to the GP/nurse or because it is easy to cause an embarrassed youngster to withdraw if the doctor is seen to be in a hurry?

Adolescents are often tempted to produce an acceptable ticket of entry, thinking the GP likes physical conditions like a sore throat or pre-menstrual tension. This is designed to counter their embarrassment while they assess the mood of the GP or nurse and work out whether they should reveal more of their problems. Sometimes in order to save time, the GP can treat the ticket and leave no time to elicit the patient's real concern.

Language

Professionals find it hard not to use medical jargon and are often unfamiliar with the teenage vocabulary. The team might like to discuss how to turn medical words into young people's language. For example, when the GP talks of the need for 'confidentiality' the adolescent patient might translate this into 'my parents must not find out'. To them even being seen visiting the surgery or taking a prescription to the pharmacy can be a problem. How would teenagers describe words like constipation, disurea, sexual intercourse, vagina, masturbation and different recreational drugs? Lifestyles can be formed during adolescence in matters such as smoking, exercise and safe sex, but there is a temptation for professionals who are keen to encourage health promotion to give advice too early in the consultation.

Adolescents are only likely to be influenced once their problems have been addressed. Consultations primarily need to be about the patient's agenda and only secondary about the doctor's. One young woman reported after a consultation 'he only wanted to find out if I needed to go on the Pill and had stopped smoking. He doesn't seem interested in my problem'.

Strong feelings

Teenagers often stir strong feelings in adults. This can happen in any consultation leaving the GP or nurse with frustrations and uncomfortable feelings of irritation, despair or anger. A skilled professional monitors such feelings and tries to use them in the process of making a diagnosis – and avoids reacting directly to them.

The team might like to share how they do this and how they differentiate between feelings of irritation arising from issues in their own lives and those projected on to them by a disturbed young patient. Another difficulty worth discussing is how the GP/nurse avoids slipping from a professional role into a paternalistic role during a consultation. This is essentially likely to happen when the GP has cared for the patient since childhood. Changing their relationship to a more adult one may be difficult when the patient is in distress but if it is not done it can undermine the adolescent's developing autonomy and cause resentment.

Whatever an adolescent experiences when they seek help from the surgery, it is their perception of how they are treated in the consultation that decides if they return and how much they use primary care in the future. It is important from time to time for primary care teams to discuss their consultation techniques with this age group and share honestly the difficulties they may encounter. It is also advisable for the team to use each other to share difficult situations arising in the consultation as a form of in-house supervision.

Examples of ten minute consultations with teenagers

Contraception

History Susan is 16 and has been having sex with her present boyfriend for three months. She has had one scare last month where she needed emergency contraception. She is now wondering about going on the Pill in case it happens again.

Issues you should cover.

- Explore the reason for the condom failure and teach condom techniques as condoms are still very important for protection against sexually transmitted infections as well as pregnancy prevention. Ensure that she knows that if she wants to carry on using condoms she can use emergency contraception again if need be.

- Go over the pros and cons of taking the Pill and find out about her medical and family history, giving health promotion advice as appropriate.

- Explain how to take the Pill, emphasising what to do if she misses or forgets a Pill and give an information leaflet.

What you should do.

- Discuss what she knows about the Pill. Explain that the combined Pill works by stopping an egg from being released.

- Explain the advantages of the Pill, which include: 99% effective against getting pregnant if correctly used; easy to use and doesn't interfere with sex; gives regular and usually lighter periods (ask about periods); may reduce pre-menstrual syndrome (check whether PMS is a problem); protects against ovarian and endometrial cancer (check family history of these cancers).

- Explain disadvantages of the Pill, which include: lack of protection against STIs so there is a need to use condoms.

- Discuss minor/nuisance side effects, which include: headaches (check about headaches and migraines); mood changes (check for depression); weight (check weight against height); breast tenderness; breakthrough bleeding; decreased libido. Explain that you can usually find a Pill that suits, and that many of these minor problems do settle within the first few months of use.

- Discuss serious side effects: heart attacks; strokes; hypertension (check blood pressure); blood clots. Find out about family history of any of these and decide whether the Pill is appropriate for them. Explain increased risk of venous thrombosis from 5/100 000 women to 15/100 000 women in those taking 'second' generation Pill and up to 30/100 000 women taking 'third' generation Pill. Emphasise the risk of smoking and the Pill on heart attacks and strokes (take smoking history).

- Discuss cancer risks: breast cancer risk increases from 2/1000 to 3/1000 in women under 35. Check family history of breast cancer. Cervical cancer – increased risk on the Pill – probably protected by using condoms. Will need to have cervical smears from age of 20.

Susan decides she does want the Pill.

- Show her a packet of Pills and explain when to take them.
- Tell her to start the Pill on the first day of her period.
- Remind her that each month she will start the new pack on the same day of the week.
- Go over what to do if she misses a Pill, takes antibiotics or has an episode of gastroenteritis: take the next one as soon as possible, use condoms for seven days and, if missed Pills are one of the last seven in the packet, run two packs together.
- Emphasise that it is more risky to miss Pills at the beginning and the end of packs, describe how the Pill suppresses the ovaries and stops ovulation, and how the ovaries start to 'wake up' and get ready for ovulation during the Pill free days. If this time is extended then ovulation is more likely to occur.
- Use the FPS combined Pill leaflet as a written reminder, especially giving the details about missed Pills.
- Check if she has any questions.
- Prescribe a three months supply of the Pill and give her a supply of condoms.
- Arrange to see her after three months.

Make appropriate claim for family planning fee.

Depression

> **History** Richard is 16, and is brought to the practice by his mother. She says that since completing his GCSEs he has had trouble sleeping and is tired all day. She recounts how he argues about getting up in mornings, tidying his room and over doing his college work. Richard's father left the family when he was three. He has two sisters, one older, who is unmarried and has a child, and one younger, who is at school. They live in the country and Richard travels each day to sixth form college.

Issues you should cover.

- See Richard on his own and explore his version of the problem.
- Assess how long he has had difficulties.
- Take a detailed history of his symptoms:
  - sleep? He says he goes to bed at 2am and gets up at 8am
  - mood throughout the day?
  - ability to concentrate?
  - what does he enjoy in life?
  - has he thought of suicide?

What you should do.

- Listen and sympathise whilst trying to understand how Richard feels.
- Exclude any physical cause.
- Explain to Richard that people of his age can experience serious mood swings which can lift as quickly as they come, and that this is normal if it only lasts a couple of weeks. If it continues for months it can become a 'clinical depression', which needs treatment.
- If his symptoms are not too severe and have been around for a short time, suggest:
  - he does things he enjoys

- he avoids arguments with his mother but stands up for himself (i.e. treats his room as he wishes)
- he talks to friends of his own age about his troubles
- he returns to see you in one to two weeks to report on how things are going.

- If you feel that his symptoms point to a real depression, especially if he has 'suicide ideation', consider:
  - referral to an adolescent psychiatrist (this may be a very long wait)
  - antidepressants (but most antidepressants are not very effective in this age group). Choose one that will not harm if overdosed
  - counselling
  - seeing him again in a week
  - discussing his case with the local adolescent psychiatrist.

- Speak to mother in Richard's presence having cleared this with him and suggest to mother that she respects Richard's growing autonomy and avoids arguing over his room, and that it should be treated as his territory. Tell her what you plan to do and enlist her support.

Case studies

There are more cases below for which you can make up ten minute consultations, or use for team/training discussions.

Case 1 Mary, aged 16 years, consults her female GP.

Mary: '*I have acne – my mum says there is a Pill which is good for it.*'

GP: '*There is a Pill for acne – why do you think your mother has suggested it?*'

Mary: '*I have a boyfriend.*'

GP: '*Do you think your mother wants you to be a little safer?*'

No reply.

GP: '*Have you had intercourse?*'

Mary: '*Someone forced me into it …*' She looks embarrassed.

Where does the GP go from here?

Case 2 David, aged 15 years, consults with his mother. His parents separated a year ago and both have new partners.

When David is seen on his own he confirms his mother's anxiety about him not sleeping. He declares that he is worried about his mother and does not wish to add to her problems by telling her how awful he feels. On direct questioning he admits that he is thinking of suicide as a way of making life easier for his parents.

How does a doctor handle this situation?

Case 3 Roger, a West Indian boy of 14 years, has been brought to England by his mother. He is sad to have left his grandmother and friends back home and angry that his mother has married a new man who has a two-year-old step daughter. Roger has been excluded from school for the fourth time for being aggressive towards his teachers and chasing the girls. This last time he hit his teacher. The school have told his mother to take him to the GP and have said that they will not take him back until the GP has sorted out Roger and his family.

How does the GP do this?

Case 4 Ann is 15-years-old and she has a longstanding behaviour problem. She lives with her father and her aunt. They have called in her GP as Ann has confined herself in the front room and has remained there with the curtains drawn for over ten months. She is demanding and domineering towards her adult relatives and is indulging in obsessive behaviour. The local authorities have commenced care proceedings and a care order is being made for her to receive a psychiatric examination under the Children's Act.

The GP talks to Ann on her own and finds she understands the situation and what is proposed. The GP assesses her as competent. Ann refuses to give consent to seeing a psychiatrist or to being moved.

What does the GP do next?

Case 5 A nurse and health visitor running a teenage drop-in centre in the practice sees a 15-year-old Asian girl called Nitali.

The patient asks for reassurance that what she tells the nurse will not be repeated to any of the family. The nurse promises that everything heard in the clinic is confidential. Nitali then bursts into tears and tells the nurse how her uncle 'babysits' for her and her two younger sisters whenever her parents go out. He has, she says, for some time sexually abused her on these occasions. She is frightened that he will start doing this to her sisters as they are both growing up very quickly.

What should the nurse do?

Case 6 A 17-year-old patient with fibrocystic disease has been treated by a paediatric department all his life. He consults his GP saying that he does not want to be transferred to an adult department in a different hospital as he does not want to lose his consultant or the paediatric unit where he is well known.

He then says that he has a girlfriend whose parents are unhappy about their relationship. He asks 'Is there any danger that if I marry her our children will develop CF like me?'.

What does the GP say?

Case 7 Margaret, aged 16, came for emergency contraception ten days ago. She returns because she has not yet had a period and her partner split the condom the previous night. She is unsure of the date of her last 'normal' period, but thinks it was about three weeks ago. Her cycle is usually irregular – between three and six weeks she thinks.

How should the nurse handle it? What are the options?

Case 8 Dan is 14-years-old. He is of Afro-Caribbean origin and has lived alone with his mother from infancy. He has well controlled asthma and attends the asthma clinic annually. The nurse has known Dan for many years as he started attending the clinic before he started school.

Last year he attended the clinic on his own. The usual topics concerning asthma were discussed and height and weight were measured. Dan has grown into a tall and good looking lad who is popular at school and involved with sport and girls.

The measurements showed a significant increase in both height and weight. A discussion followed whereby the nurse and Dan explored diet and lifestyle issues. Dan's mother worked full time and after school Dan was expected to go to his grandmother's house until his mother returned. He was taking this opportunity to visit fast food outlets and roam the streets with his friends. Dan was able to express some of his concerns regarding his home situation.

A few days later, Dan's mother came to the surgery to see the nurse and expressed her concern with the consultation. Her fear was that Dan might become obsessed with his weight and felt that the consultation had raised unnecessary anxiety.

This case could raise the following issues:

- The value of chronic disease management to build relationships.
- Confidentiality with under 16-year-olds.
- Time issues in consultations with teenagers. Do nurses have more time than doctors?
- On-going support.
- Meeting parents' needs.

Case 9 Maria is a bright and bubbly 17-year-old. She lives with her parents, who are traditional Italian. Her boyfriend is older, they have been together since Maria was 15. Maria is a strong willed girl who lives a somewhat chaotic lifestyle and struggles with the strict atmosphere at home. She has a good relationship with an aunt, who has accompanied Maria to the surgery. All the family are registered at the surgery. Maria has been using the contraceptive injection Depo Provera. For most of the time since starting the injection she has been amenorrhoeic. Attending for her last injection she mentioned some spot bleeding that she has been experiencing over the past two months. The nurse thought it necessary to take a high vaginal swab. The result showed gonorrhoea. The boyfriend had been away travelling on business. Both were referred to the local specialist clinic.

This case could raise the following issues:

- Supporting adolescents in their choice of contraception.
- Confidentiality.
- Raising difficult issues.
- Sensitivity with invasive examinations.
- Talking about safe sex.
- Delivering the message of healthy lifestyle.
- Raising self-esteem.
- Coping with relationships.

Case 10 A 15-year-old lad who had been invited to attend the surgery to see a nurse for a health check expressed concerns about his father's drinking habit. The parents had recently divorced and the boy was living with his mother in the family home and visiting his father at weekends. He was concerned that his father often seemed to have been drinking heavily and would insist on driving the car, taking his son with him.

This case could raise the following issues:

- Medico-legal issues.
- Supporting the adolescent.

- Referral agencies.
- Managing the consultation.
- Empowering the adolescent.
- Accessing adolescents so that they can attend the surgery – how do we do it?

Chapter 7

The role of the primary care nurse

The whole of this manual applies to nurses and doctors working in primary care, however this chapter deals with some specific roles that nurses can play when dealing with adolescents.

The primary care team liaises with many different types of community nurses whose salary is paid for by others. These include health visitors, district nurses and specialist nurses in the community. Readers will know all about these nurses so we will just touch upon their function in order to remind the reader of the contributions they can make.

Practice nurses

Nurses are essential to the running of our primary care services. Many nurses have a personal interest in helping adolescents and the skills to build up trusting relationships with them. Every primary care team should ask itself whether they are fully utilising the skills that the nurses in their practice and community are offering in the care of the teenagers on their list.

A practice nurse's most helpful contribution takes place while undertaking their routine clinical work, i.e. when seeing young people for immunisation, sports injury, wound dressing, etc. In this situation the nurse can build a relationship of trust with her young patient and this can be used to:

- encourage appropriate use of the surgery
- provide simple health education with things like diet, smoking or sexual health
- open up underlying worries or psychological problems.

In addition, some practice nurses are prepared to take on responsibility for providing additional help to the primary care team, i.e.

- supply and display of leaflets/posters appropriate for teenagers
- seeing adolescents who request an urgent appointment when no general practitioner is available
- supporting receptionists who are stumped by an adolescent problem
- liaising with local school nurses
- organising primary care meetings to discuss adolescent problems including difficulties over confidentiality and consultations.

Specialist trained nurses may be pleased to take a lead role in organising and running clinics which adolescents could attend. Such as:

- an asthma or diabetic clinic
- a vaccination or travel clinic
- a sexual health clinic
- a quit smoking clinic
- a teenage clinic.

For the practice nurse to make their maximum contribution to adolescent care, it is important that they have an open dialogue with the primary care team about how services are run, problems that arise and how adolescent care can be expanded.

School nurses

School nurses seem to deliver a creative, holistic and proactive service to their school aged population. They are often the first health professional a young person can directly self-refer to for support and advice on a health related issue.

School nurses are specialist practitioners, public health nurses and primary healthcare providers. The key roles of school nurses are to provide health advice and support to young people of school age by working with young people individually, in small groups, alongside teachers in the classroom, to deliver health promotion in areas such as sex and relationships, self-esteem and mental health promotion.

School nurses either have a proactive contact with clients or are the first point of contact for a child with an identified health problem and can refer on to other professionals as appropriate.

School nurses are ideally placed to develop multi-agency partnerships with GPs, the primary healthcare team and other agencies to promote the health of the local population. This aspect of their work is something which needs to be developed and capitalised upon to ensure that young people are able to access the kind of health services they want and to ensure that appropriate liaison between health professionals is maintained to meet the health needs of young people safely and consistently. It is also important to share and value the unique contributions and skills that all professionals have to offer young people within primary healthcare.

School nurses are the key link between health and education services to support links operationally and to strategically implement the public health and ill health prevention agenda.

Health visitors

Some of these are attached to practices and others to geographical areas. All are responsible for health promotion. It is up to primary care teams to make the effort to work closely with health visitors to get their support for the work the surgery undertakes in promoting health to the adolescents and their families in the local community.

District nurses

In their capacity as visitors to patients' homes to provide post-operative care, wound dressings, injections, etc., these nurses can be of help with teenagers suffering from serious conditions who are sent home from hospital and looked after at home.

Specialist nurses

There are now many specialist nurses working in the community that include those working in the following areas:

- advocacy and mental disordered offenders
- addiction nursing community orientated approach
- palliative care
- dermatology nursing
- community nursing services for people with learning disabilities
- community children's nursing.

All of these could be helpful to the primary care team and it is important that each team discovers what is available in their local community and liaises with them as best as possible.

General Practice Nursing Specialist Practitioner Programmes cover the following areas:

- health promotion and interventions for the whole practice population

- the assessment of interventions relating to women's health
- management of clinical conditions and development of strategies to affect appropriate nursing interventions
- health needs analysis of practice population
- palliative care
- the role of the practice nurse and the prevention, recognition and early intervention of substance misuse
- the use of a variety of diagnostic tools within agreed protocols
- immunisation, travel advice and vaccination
- knowledge of mental illness and interventions
- assessments and meeting the needs of vulnerable people and those at risk of mental illness.

All of these are relevant to the care of adolescents.

Chapter 8

Example of protocol and guidelines for issuing emergency contraception for young people in primary care

Patient's name ....   Date of birth .../.../......

Date and time of unprotected intercourse?	....

Was it more than 72 hours ago?	Yes/No
Any other episodes since her last period?	Yes/No
If so, were any of these more than 72 hours ago?	Yes/No

If there was any risk of conception more than 72 hours ago, discuss with doctor.

Approximate date of last period?	....
Was this a normal period?	Yes/No

If LMP was not normal, or if time since LMP is longer than usual for her, and there is a chance she may already be pregnant, discuss with doctor.

Is the risk of pregnancy due to missed
contraceptive Pills?   Yes/No

If yes, take details of which Pill she is on, which Pills she has missed,
and discuss with doctor.

Personal medical history

Serious or past illness/operation	Yes/No
Unexplained vaginal bleeding	Yes/No
Current breast feeding	Yes/No
Previous problems with emergency contraception	Yes/No
Allergic to progesterones	Yes/No

Discuss with doctor if any of the above answers are 'yes'.

BP .... if over 140/90 advise a later check with GP.

Current medication

If currently taking anti-epileptic, anti-TB or anti-fungal medication,
refer to doctor. If on any other new or unfamiliar medication check
this in the British National Formulary and discuss with doctor if
there is any mention of an interaction with hormonal contraception.

Counselling

Give information leaflet and discuss as necessary. If she is under 16,
advise her to discuss contraception with her parents. If you are concerned, give EC but discuss the situation with doctor at the earliest
opportunity.

Discussed with (name of doctor)

Levonelle 2 given to patient   Yes/No

Follow-up/additional notes/verbal instructions from doctor

Nurse's signature   Date ....
Doctor's signature   Date ....

Additional information when issuing emergency contraception

Age: discuss with doctor if under 14 or does not meet Gillick criteria.

Previous use of EC/progesterones: discuss with doctor if previously significantly unwell with EC or progesterones, previous EC failure, has already had EC since LMP, or more than three times in the last six months.

BP: discuss with doctor if at or above 140/90.

Periods: discuss with doctor if LMP not normal (may already be pregnant) or if she has had any other recent unexplained vaginal bleeding.

Risk of pregnancy: significant risk of pregnancy days 7 to 17 of 28 day cycle, midcycle pregnancy risk is about 30%, there is never no risk. Discuss with doctor if any risk of pregnancy more than 72 hours ago, or if assault/rape.

Missed Pills: Combined Pill – there is a risk if she had unprotected intercourse in the seven days after missing either two or more Pills from the first seven Pills in the pack **or** four or more Pills from the middle seven days of the pack **or** two or more Pills from the last seven days of the pack and has not run the pack straight on **or** various Pills at different times in the pack **or** Pills at the end of one pack and beginning of the next resulting in a Pill free interval of more than eight days. Progesterone only Pill – there is a risk if she has had unprotected intercourse in the seven days after taking any Pill more than three hours late.

Instructions: she may omit the contraceptive Pill which would be taken at the same time as the EC. She should then continue Pill taking as usual, plus condoms for seven days. If the EC is given during the last seven days of a combined oral contraceptive (COC) pack, run the next pack straight on. Advise her to return for a routine pregnancy test in three weeks as she may have a withdrawal bleed even if the EC were to have failed.

Medical history: discuss with doctor if there are any significant positive findings, breast feeding, or if the patient is taking enzyme inducing drugs. Any new or unfamiliar drugs should be checked in the British National Formulary and discussed with the doctor if there is any mention of interaction with hormonal contraception.

Counselling: (offer current Family Planning Service EC information leaflet).

Regime: suggest treatment is started as soon as feasible.

Side effects: emphasise safety of treatment. Side effects are unlikely, except for nausea, advise taking Pills with food and no alcohol, must see doctor if vomiting occurs within two hours of either dose. Anti-emetics need not be given routinely. If the patient is anxious to avoid symptoms or had symptoms with previous use of EC, advise ordinary travel sickness tablets. Anti-emetics can either be taken with the first dose of EC, or wait and see whether symptoms occur.

Possible failure: if taken correctly, the pregnancy rate with Levonorgestrel EC is about 1%, with IUCD it is even lower. If patient wishes to consider an IUCD, discuss with doctor. Advise her to return for a pregnancy test if she does not have a normal period within two weeks of the expected date, or in three weeks if periods are very irregular.

Risk to pregnancy: extremely unlikely that EC would affect a pregnancy. Explain if necessary that no pregnancy is completely risk free. EC acts before implantation and is not a termination of pregnancy.

Protection for rest of cycle: stress the need for this, offer condoms. Consider the need for an STD risk investigation/future protection, offer information as appropriate.

Future contraception: check plans and give information on methods as appropriate; refer if there are problems. If she wants to start a COC it may be better to make another appointment. If she wishes to restart COC, and this has been prescribed by one of the doctors in the last 24 months, then reissue according to usual guidelines for oral contraception. Start Pills on third day of proper bleeding and use condoms for the first seven days. Discuss with doctor if any significant findings in the COC protocol.

Follow-up: only needs to be seen routinely if she requires a pregnancy test, contraceptive advice, or additional support. If she has severe abdominal pains, she should see a doctor urgently.

Prescription: give prescription for ....

Chapter 9

Health promotion tips

Adolescent/young person/teenager is from the beginning of the 10th year to the end of the 19th year.

Health is 'the ability to resist the strains and stresses of a physical, mental and social nature, so that they do not lead to a reduction in life span, function or well-being'.

Health promotion is any deliberate intervention aimed at increasing 'the ability to resist the strains and stresses of a physical, mental and social nature, so that they do not lead to a reduction in life span, function or well-being'.

Effective health promotion intervention means that there is some research evidence that such an intervention has a significant effect on health in the direction desired at some time during the entire life span of the recipient of such an intervention.

- '*What should I be doing about my health?*' is not going to be first thought passing through a teenager's mind when s/he wakes up each morning. More likely it will be '*Headache, drank too much last night: did I use contraception? What homework have I got to have in today? Hell, it can't be that time already*', etc., etc.

- Society as a whole has the main responsibility for the health of young people, e.g. the availability and price of cigarettes.

- Individual young people have responsibilities for their health, e.g. using contraception when having sex, visiting the surgery when they need immunisations, not drinking and driving, etc.

- Certain health related activities in adolescents, like smoking, will have a significant long term effect on health.

- Other health related activities, like exercise, may also have a short term effect on young people's health.

Factors that influence young people's health related behaviours are complicated and include:

- genetic influences on both physique and behaviours

- the need for survival in a rapidly changing society

- the socio-economic environment in which the child/adolescent grows up

- cultural factors relating to the child's/adolescent's background and present environment

- physical and psychological changes relating to puberty

- the influences of the media and advertising

- parental influences

- influences relating to gender

- peer group influences

- the media.

Major stakeholders in the behaviour of young people include:

- young people themselves, parents and other members of society as a whole

- companies with direct financial interests in young people as a potential market, e.g. for cigarettes, clothes, toys, electronic games, foods, magazines, books, etc.

- television, magazines, papers, etc.

- schools and primary, secondary and tertiary healthcare providers.

Given these factors what do we know about effective interventions?

The effectiveness of health promotion interventions to young people is under researched – but what evidence there is suggests that:

- pricing policies are effective, particularly in the field of tobacco use by adolescents
- advertising does affect young people, what they buy and how they behave
- simultaneous multi-dimensional interventions at a national, local and individual level are more effective than individual health promotion at any one level
- health promotion at primary care level can be effective, particularly if it relates to a specific health problem suffered by the person whose health behaviour is to be changed.

What is the role of primary healthcare in health promotion to young people?

- Providing up-to-date evidence-based data for young people via such sources as the web, e.g. www.teenagehealthfreak.org and leaflets designed specifically for young people, including a 'practice' leaflet about what the practice provides for young people.
- Advising young people about health risks when they consult on related problems, i.e. smoking and a chest infection.
- Supporting multi-dimensional campaigns at national, local and individual level, e.g. against cigarette smoking.
- Providing easy access for adolescents to health related facilities like contraception.
- Supporting educational initiatives which promote self-confidence and self-esteem in young people.
- Supporting political initiatives, like raising the price of cigarettes.
- Making sure all young people in the practice know how to use the health services, e.g. how to register as a temporary patient,

how to get an appointment, how and where to get contraceptive advice including emergency contraception (any GP, young people's clinics, etc.).

Chapter 10

Adolescent clinics

Different models

- 'Drop in clinics' that are run in the practice and deal either with all aspects of adolescent health or specific issues, e.g. sexual health.
- 'Booked clinics' that are run in the practice and deal with either general adolescent or specific adolescent health issues.
- 'School based clinics' that are run by primary care doctors and/or nurses.
- 'Drop in clinics' that are held in a purpose developed clinic away from the practice or a school.
- 'Birthday call up' are appointments that are made by the practice around patient's 16th birthday.

Issues to consider when setting up an adolescent clinic

At present there does not appear to be an agreement about the best way of providing these services for young people. Most agree that the following issues need to be borne in mind.

- There needs to be a key figure who is enthusiastic about the project.

- Ongoing funding needs to be considered.
- The style of the clinics needs to be considered.
- The style of the clinics needs to be shaped on the characteristics and requirements of the local population of young people and to take account of other local services.
- Evaluation of the project needs to be considered from the start.

Some tips for setting up an adolescent clinic yourself

- Why do you think that the practice needs a specialist adolescent clinic?
- Have you undertaken a 'needs assessment'?
- Should it be done in cooperation with a group of other local practices?
- What other facilities exist for adolescents locally?
- What are the aims and objectives of the new services?
- Who is the key person who is going to lead the new services?
- What specifically are you going to offer in the clinic?
- Where and when will it be held?
- How are you going to involve teenagers in setting it up?
- How will you advertise it to teenagers?
- Where will funding come from?
- How will you evaluate it? (Number attending, satisfaction, what problems arise, etc.).

GP adolescent clinic

These are most often open only to those registered with the practice. Many send an appointment to those on the practice list on their 16th birthday (some on their 12th or 13th birthday). Patients are asked to ring the receptionist if the time of the appointment is inconvenient to arrange an alternative appointment. Some practices include a letter for the young person's parents.

The invitation is to update the patient's records, check on their immunisation status and general health and discuss any problems they may have. Some of these clinics have produced a 50–60% response (the records of those who do not respond can be marked so they can be interviewed when next seen). Clinics held once a week can accept drop ins by leaving some appointment times open – these can be used for return visits or for patients who have a new problem that they wish to discuss.

Many attempts by practices to start such clinics have failed, but others have succeeded. What factors make the difference is still not known.

Setting up a clinic in or near to a local school

Why? Confidential access to the surgery can be difficult for some young people because of travel difficulties or because of the fear of meeting neighbours, or relatives, at the surgery.

School is the one place that all 12–16-year-olds must attend and where, strangely, they can have some privacy.

Links with the school nurse can provide a coordinated approach to setting up a clinic that young people can attend by being given a ticket by the school.

Where to hold it? A suitable room may be found on the school site. It needs a waiting area out of view of other pupils, or staff, and one or two consulting rooms. The room needs to be adequately equipped, e.g. couch, height measure, scales, and it needs a secure place to store records, etc.

If no suitable accommodation is found in the school, a nearby hospital, surgery, or youth centre may be adequate and even preferable in that it is perceived by the pupils to be distinct from school. If this option is chosen, a system of passes to allow access to pupils can be devised. It is important to strike a balance so that the system is secure from the school's point of view but that no questions are asked from the pupil's point of view.

Other stakeholders. Setting up a clinic in or near a school necessitates interacting with and bringing on board the many agencies involved – pupils, parents, teachers, governors, school nurse, GPs, etc. Each of these groups will have its own concerns. Pupils need to be involved in the project at an early stage, so that they feel ownership of it. A health needs survey can help them to feel that their voice is important. A competition to name the clinic or to design posters can stimulate interest. Each pupil can be given a credit card with details of the clinic and other useful information. The clinic needs to be easily accessible without embarrassment. Pupils must be certain that it is safe space.

GPs in several practices may have pupils at a given school. Historically GPs have been very averse to other doctors seeing their patients but the advent of co-ops has challenged this. The most local practices may link together to cover the clinic. More distant practices may be asked to give permission for their patients to be seen at the clinic and to take part in the rota if they want to. This cooperation will raise prescribing issues. The prescribing authority in Newcastle can set up a prescribing pad for the clinic's use if funding for the budget can be organised at a local level.

Head and teachers may be concerned about the disruption of lessons, about pupils leaving the school site, about discipline problems being medicalised. Meeting with them can deal with these concerns. A potential advantage to the teaching staff is that when pupils come to them with difficult problems, because of the educational department rules they are supposed to pass information on. With a clinic, the teacher can say 'don't say anymore to me, go to see the doctor/school nurse'. He/she is then relieved of a difficult dilemma.

Parents may be very suspicious of doctors other than their own GP seeing their children. They may also feel that they will be undermined. A health survey of pupils prior to setting up this type of clinic assessed their current use of their GP surgery. It showed that the main concerns were stress, bullying, relationships, etc., and not contraception and sexually transmitted diseases. These results were presented to the parents at an open meeting where any remaining concerns were addressed. The commissioning group of the PCGPCT may be able to provide some funding and help with prescribing issues.

Records. There are two issues here.

1 Records need to be kept in the clinic. This is particularly important if different doctors are going to be involved in the running of the clinic. Arrangements need to be made for these to be kept securely. Some thought needs to be put into what information to record, e.g. past medical history, own GP, tutor at school, current medication and allergies, parental contact information, consent to make contact with parent/guardian, own GP tutor, etc.

2 There needs to be a system for getting information back to the patient's notes at the surgery. This can be done by email, by computer link, by letter, by fax or by 'phone. Ongoing evaluation can then be made from the records.

Examples of existing clinics for young people

Tic-Tac is a primary care drop in advice and information centre situated in a secondary school in Cornwall. It mainly covers sexual health. Significant partners include the local healthcare trust, primary healthcare teachers, community education, school governors, parents and young people.

It is staffed by GPs, health visitors, practice nurses and midwifes. The project has been well evaluated and has been found to provide a relevant, accessible, confidential service which responds to the needs of the young people it serves.

A yearly report is produced which shows continued growth of the service.

Burnham Medical Centre Clinic was started by the practice nurse. The aim is to give young people in the area ongoing support and education so that they may take responsibility for their healthcare and life style.

The clinic is open one evening a week from 6pm–8pm and is available to under 20-year-olds regardless of whether they are registered as a patient.

The clinic is staffed by a practice nurse – who is also a counsellor – two GPs and a 'friendly' receptionist. After a slow start, data shows that numbers attending have steadily increased to about 20 per session which, if it continues, will require more staff.

The Brent Young Persons Centre is a charity started 33 years ago to help suicidal young people. It offered psychotherapy by well trained psychiatrists, and carried out research into the factors that cause emotional distress in this age group.

Today, with the help of statutory funding, this charity also offers careers advice and support with problems in sexual health and drugs and alcohol. It has a member of staff who goes out to local schools to work with young people who have problems.

Chapter 11

Health related questions commonly asked by young people

A sample of young people aged 10–19 years were asked to list the three questions they would most like to ask their doctor or another health professional. The top ten topics and examples of questions are as below.

1 **Contraception**
   - How do I know what is best for me?
   - Where do I go?
   - At what age can I take the Pill?

2 **Period problems**
   - Why are periods so painful?
   - Why aren't they regular?
   - What can I do about heavy bleeding?

3 **Weight**
   - How can I lose weight?
   - What is the ideal weight for my height?

4 **Exercise/healthy eating**
   - What is the best form of exercise?
   - How can I find out about a healthy diet?

5 Sex

- Where can I go to get good information about sex?
- Does sex at a young age increase the risk of disease?
- Should we allow ourselves to be pushed into having sex?

6 Confidentiality

- Can I trust my doctor to keep what I tell him/her confidential?
- Is there anything they will tell my mum about?
- Do they discuss patients with their colleagues?

7 Sexually transmitted diseases

- How can I protect myself from AIDS?
- How can I tell if I have a STD?
- Is my vaginal discharge normal?

8 Acne

- Is there a cure for it?
- Does eating chocolate cause spots?
- Do any of the creams work?

9 Stress and depression

- Why do I feel so stressed out?
- Does anyone care about me?
- Why does love hurt so much?

10 Cancer

- How can I protect myself from cancer?
- What are the early signs of cancer?
- Can a doctor tell straight away if I've got cancer?

Source: Jones R, Finlay F, Simpson N, Kreitman T (1997) How can adolesecents' health needs and concerns best be met? *Br J Gen Prac.* **47:** 631–4.

The anonymous health dialogue with teenagers

An analysis of 1500 health related questions asked by teenagers from a virtual surgery website www.teenagehealthfreak.org, showed the following.

- **Serious sexual questions (including contraception) – 26%**
  Dear Dr Ann, I think I masturbate too much. From anon …
  and
  Dear Dr Ann, how do I know if I am gay?

- **Sexual nonsense – 18.5%**
  Dear Dr Ann, my willie is three foot long and my girlfriend says she thinks that it may hurt her …

- **Diet, weight – 7%**
  Dear Dr Ann, I am 61.6 kg and 5 foot 4 inches tall. Do I need to lose any weight or am I normal weight? I am 14-years-old.

- **Minor illnesses, e.g. nose bleeds, coughs, colds, headaches, etc. – 5%**
  Dear Dr Ann – I'm fifteen and I get these headaches which come on when I'm stressed. But what worries me is that I get these funny spots in my eyes and then …

- **Puberty – 2%**
  Dear Dr Ann, I'm 14 and 5'5" but I haven't got any hair down there and all my mates have. When will it start? From 'hairless worried'.

- **Relationships – 5%**
  Dear Dr Ann, I think that my parents are getting divorced. I heard my mum shouting at my dad that she wants him to get out. I am afraid I am going to be left all alone, and I don't know who to talk to about it. Feeling very lonely, aged 14.

- **Smoking – 5%**
  Dear Dr Ann, if you try a fag do you get addicted straight away? And how many fags does it take to get addicted?

- **Body image, e.g. hairiness, small breasts, size of penis – 3.5%**
  Dear Dr Ann, my penis is a lot smaller than that of the average size, can you tell me what to do, please, please help me I am really scared but daren't go to the doctor ...

Chapter 12

Papers concerning teenage health

These papers represent the most salient recent research and assessment of the health of teenagers when viewed from a primary care perspective.

1 McPherson A, Macfarlane A and Allen J (1996) What do young people want from their GP? *Br J Gen Prac.* **46:** 627.
   This is a short report listing the opinions of students aged 16 and 17 years from schools in Oxfordshire. Their responses indicated that concerns about confidentiality were paramount, and also indicated young people's clinics and 'phone advice would be helpful.

2 Kari J, Donovan C, Li J and Taylor B (1997) Adolescents' attitudes to general practice in North London. *Br J Gen Prac.* **47:** 109–10.
   Another school-based project, with a larger sample, and looking at ages 12 to 18 years. Quicker appointments, friendlier receptionists, and more sympathetic doctors emerged as themes of concern to teenagers in this study.

3 Jones R, Finlay F, Simpson N and Kreitman T (1997) How can adolescents' health needs and concerns best be met? *Br J Gen Prac.* **47:** 631–4.
   Another school-based survey, but also involving replies to a survey in a popular teenage magazine. Thoughts about a more

'user-friendly' service were expressed, and included 'wish lists' of 'ideal' surgeries and doctors. It is certainly clear that many do not match up to the ideal.

4 Donovan C, Mellanby A, Jacobson L *et al.* (1997) Members of the Adolescent Working Party, RCGP. Teenagers' views on the GP consultation and their provision of contraception. *Br J Gen Prac.* **47:** 715–18.
A very large school survey. Issues of confidentiality, embarrassment, unsympathetic GPs, and difficulties in getting quick appointments again feature as causes of concern to 15 and 16-year-olds.

5 Gregg R, Freeth D and Blackie C (1998) Teenage health and the practice nurse: choice and opportunity for both? *Br J Gen Prac.* **48:** 909–10.
A survey of GP practice nurses in London. Most were seeing teenagers, but many felt undertrained and unsupported in their care of teenagers. Discussion about alcohol, confidentiality, and psychosocial issues caused most discomfort to practice nurses.

6 Jacobson L, Mellanby A, Donovan C *et al.* (2002) Members of the Adolescent Working Party, RCGP. Teenagers' views on general practice consultations and other medical advice. *Fam Prac.* **17:** 156–8.
A follow-up survey showing that teenage views on GP services indicated a more favourable series of opinions on GP care. However, it still shows high levels of dissatisfaction with services, and many teenagers who report they do not approach GP services for help because they do not feel the services respect them as patients.

7 Kramer T and Garralda M (1998) Psychiatric disorders in adolescents in primary care. *Br J Psych.* **173:** 508–13.
A very good review of the mental health of teenagers in primary care. GPs are relatively poor at recognising and managing adolescent distress. Pointers might include frequent

consultations, history of bullying or other stress. Screening for depression is possible, but has problems, and the authors recognise the difficulties of providing high quality primary care to distressed teenagers. An important aspect of future research work.

8 Churchill R, Allen J, Denman S *et al.* (2000) Do the attitudes and beliefs of young teenagers towards general practice influence actual consultation behaviour? *Br J Gen Prac.* **50:** 953–7.
Interestingly, this paper from Nottingham reports less of an effect in consultation behaviour than might be implied from many of the surveys above. However, the most obvious effect concerns consultations for distress and contraceptive advice, two of the potentially more worrying aspects of teenage health.

9 Hippisley-Cox J, Allen J, Pringle M *et al.* (2000) Association between teenage pregnancy rates and the age and sex of general practitioners: cross sectional survey in Trent 1994–1997. *BMJ.* **320:** 842–5.
The headline finding of this paper is that GP surgeries that have younger, female doctors tend to have lower rates of teenage pregnancy. It is important to ask why this may be, and what characteristics make older GPs less 'approachable' to teenagers.

10 Sanci L, Coffey C, Veit F *et al.* (2000) Evaluation of an educational intervention for general practitioners in adolescent health care: randomised controlled trial. *BMJ.* **320:** 224–9.
The headline finding from this paper from Australia is that training works. GPs in the state of Victoria were randomised to receive training involving simulated patients, or to receive no overt training in teenage health; the 'trained' group felt more confident and skilled when dealing with teenagers. The sting in the tail is that some of the simulated patients noted no obvious changes!

11 Ramrakha S, Caspi A, Dickson N *et al.* (2000) Psychiatric disorders and risky sex in young adulthood: a cross sectional study in a birth cohort. *BMJ.* **321:** 263–6.
This New Zealand paper reports that those with any psychiatric diagnosis indulge in risky sexual activity to a greater extent than control patients. Previous work has demonstrated an association between overdose and termination of pregnancy. A salient lesson is to consider sexual health and mental health together in the primary medical care of teenagers.

12 Jacobson L, Richardson G, Parry-Langdon N and Donovan C (2001) How do teenagers and primary healthcare providers view each other? An overview of key themes. *Br J Gen Prac.* **51:** 811–16.
This paper from the South Wales valleys is the first paper to look at the views of primary care providers and their teenage patients. It also involved a large amount of qualitative research methodology, and delineated more issues than revealed by questionnaires alone. In essence, it revealed that teenagers and providers do not always refer to the same thing when they respectively discuss such issues as confidentiality, communication or health.

13 Walker Z and Townsend J (1999) The role of general practice in promoting teenage health: a review of the literature. *Fam Prac.* **16:** 164–72.
The best recent review paper in relation to health advice as provided by GPs and others in primary care. The take-home message is that teenagers rarely receive advice, that there is a need for such activity to take place, but there is a need for research to discover effective and efficacious means of delivering such health advice.

14 Walker Z and Townsend J (1998) Promoting adolescent mental health in primary care: a review of the literature. *J Adoles.* **21:** 621–34.

In many ways, a sister paper to the above review paper. The review indicates that primary care offers a setting for the prevention and detection of mental health problems in adolescents. However, as before, more research is needed to fulfil this potential.

15   Bernard P, Garralda E, Hughes T and Tylee A (1999) Evaluation of a teaching package in adolescent psychiatry for general practitioner registrars. *Ed Gen Prac.* **10:** 21–8.
This is a study which again demonstrates that teaching and education about teenage health is feasible and that it works. In this instance, the training was for GP registrars, and showed improvements in skills, competencies and confidence in recognising and managing adolescent distress.

16   Burack R (2000) Young teenagers' attitudes towards general practitioners and their provision of healthcare. *Br J Gen Prac.* **50:** 550–4.
A paper from London demonstrating, by use of a survey of 13- to 15-year-olds in schools, that there is a lot of misinformation apparent within the community. Many were unaware that GPs had any skills in providing contraceptive services, or that people could be under 16 years of age to be seen for contraceptive services, or that GP services are confidential. A theme of poor 'marketing' of primary care services for teenagers is apparent.

17   Jacobson L and Kinnersley P (2000) Teenagers in primary care – continuing the new direction. *Br J Gen Prac.* **50:** 947–8.
The most recent editorial on teenage health and primary care. We have come a long way in the last seven years since an earlier review article, and teenage health is definitely 'on the map' as a general health issue of concern to primary care. However, there is still much to do, and the work must go on.

Chapter 13

Supporting the role of the parents

Parents are the primary healthcare providers to their children and young people 24 hours a day, 365 days a year. They need support in this role and below are some suggestions and discussion points for adolescent issues when talking to parents.

Their teenager's developing sexuality.

- Talk about sex and contraception when your children are young enough to be curious (ages 7, 8, 9 and 10) and not too old to be embarrassed (from 11 onwards).

- If you find the subject of sex too embarrassing, don't despair – you are not alone and most adults are not even very good at talking to each other about it – try getting some good books about sex and contraception which you can 'discreetly' leave around.

- Find out what the school is teaching them about sex, contraception and sexually transmitted infections so at least you are aware of any major gaps.

- You can't dictate who they go out with and too much disapproval may well keep the unwanted relationship going.

- Teenage magazines are a useful source of information about sex but do not be too shocked!

- Education and ambition are the best contraception but you can leave condoms around – though they will probably insist that they want to buy their own.

Their teenagers and the drugs scene.

- Discuss the simple end of drug facts with your child around the age of nine or earlier and keep on discussing them as they (and you) get older.

- Be at least a bit informed about the effects of drugs and why people take them.

- Believe the research that shows that if you provide young people with facts about drugs earlier it *does* delay them experimenting with drugs.

- Discuss with them why you do not want them taking drugs in your house (you could be implicated which could mean you getting arrested which would not be good for their source of financial support!).

- Do not think that your child (of either sex) will be different and will necessarily be the one *not* experimenting with illegal drugs.

- If your child gets into trouble steer a course which supports them (you have to go on living with them and they have the right to expect that support) and that at the same time aids others in performing their duty.

Moodiness, stress, anxiety and depression in their teenagers.

- Find time to talk about emotions and feelings with your children, both boys and girls.

- Moodiness, bad temper, headaches, feeling tired all the time, feeling unable to face people, sleeping problems, getting disorganised and finding it difficult to finish things may be part of being normal, but if they are interfering with a young person's life it may also mean that they are depressed, stressed or anxious.

- Seek help if your teenager's problems have lasted longer than you would expect and/or other people have commented on it.

- Realise you being stressed can cause stresses for your teenager.

- Show an interest in what they are doing and what is making them stressed – words of support are more valuable than criticisms.
- If you think (or know) the problem is school related, talk to the school to find out if they are aware of any problems – your son or daughter might be reluctant to let you know about bullying or work difficulties.

Teenagers with eating disorders.

- Refusing to sit and have meals with the family, along with demanding to eat different foods, may be early warning signs.
- Watch out for disappearance of food from the fridge and money to fund the binges if bulimia is the problem.
- Look out for regular smell of vomit in the bathroom, especially after meals.
- The earlier a young person with an eating problem gets help, especially those with anorexia, then the less likely it is to become a major problem.
- If your teenager agrees to see the doctor, realise the consultation will be confidential but it may be helpful to let the doctor know about your concerns or fears even if the communication cannot be two-way.
- Try to arrange to have regular meals where all the family sit down together and try to make sure that you keep eating normally yourself.
- Don't force high calorie foods, be supportive but firm and continue to show affection and try to avoid making them feel guilty.

Teenagers who appear to be suicidal.

- Mistrust the belief that someone who talks about suicide won't do it – it is just not true.
- If you have any fear that your teenager is suicidal, talk to your GP about it urgently.

- Value yourself and your teenager for what you are, not for what you wish you were.
- Listen to teenagers and show them that their opinions matter and are worth being heard.
- Give them responsibility and praise them when they take it rather than damning them when they don't.
- Share your concerns about your teenager with others – partners, friends, teachers, relations – most will have, or will have had, the same problems down the line.

Teenagers with chronic illness.

- Remember that a teenager with any chronic illness is, first and foremost, a person and not a disease and should always be treated as normally as possible.
- Most young people who have a chronic disorder or disability cope with adolescence and the transition to being an adult as well or as badly as any other young person.
- Recognise that there are fewer positive role models for young people with disabilities.
- Make an early start in encouraging and allowing the young person to be in charge of their illness, make them responsible for their own medication, and get them to arrange their own doctors and hospital appointments, and to take part in the choices about their illness.
- Parents are likely to find it more difficult to relinquish control and the caring role when someone has been very dependent during their childhood years. They need to take control of their disability and this needs to be balanced against the safety of their care.
- Remember a teenager with a disability will need help with all the things a teenager without a disability needs – advice and help about sex, drugs and contraception – but they will also want privacy.

Chapter 14

Developing a practice personal and professional development plan

> **The aim of the practice personal and professional development plan is to:**
>
> - ensure the practice understands the 'health needs' of the adolescent population that the practice serves
> - ensure that all members of the practice team are adequately trained to meet these needs
> - make the practice more user-friendly to all adolescents who attend
> - reduce unwanted teenage pregnancies, suicides, eating disorders, etc.

Justifying why this topic is a practice and professional priority.

- A significant proportion of practice patients are teenagers.
- Teenagers may present with emergency problems (e.g. drug overdose, family problems, depression, etc.) when other services are not available.

- Many teenagers do not know how to use the health services appropriately.

- Parents and schools frequently find teenage health problems and psychological problems too difficult to manage themselves.

Who could be included in the practice based plan? Consider including GPs, practice nurses, health visitors, social workers, receptionists, practice manager, young people and parents.

Where is the practice now with respect to adolescent services (baseline information)?

- Use the two audit sheets that are available in this book on 'How does your practice rate with teenagers?' and 'Confidentiality' (pages 3–4 and 23–4).

- Document the number of teenage pregnancies, terminations, teenage suicides, attempted suicides, known teenage drug abusers in the practice in five years.

- Contact local Department of Public Health for statistics as appropriate.

- Compare rates of individual GPs within the practice on emergency contraceptive Pill prescribing, including what guidelines they use.

Assessing the learning needs of members of the practice team.

- Hold a practice team meeting to discuss services available to teenagers in the practice.

- At the meeting discuss training needed to meet gaps in the services.

- Use case scenarios to highlight learning needs of individuals in the practice team (e.g. 15-year-old girl wanting an urgent appointment when there are none available, or do a critical incident analysis of a 14-year-old girl from an ethnic minority background presenting with a 20 week pregnancy, or a 17-year-old boy with learning difficulties wanting to discuss the problems of his epilepsy and finding a job).

- Review availability of in-house training versus local courses, etc. to meet needs.
- Identify one practice member to undertake responsibility for reviewing training needs of all other members of the team in the field of adolescent health.

Remembering to take into account the components of clinical governance.

- *Establishing a learning culture* – looking at team members' training needs.
- *Managing resources and services* – looking at adolescent needs compared with needs of other client groups and looking at possible financial returns to the practice of running teenage services.
- *Establishing a research and development culture* – getting feedback from teenagers about the services.
- *Reliable and accurate data* – making sure that you have systems within the practice to collect accurate data about adolescent health.
- *Confidentiality* – making sure that there is a written practice policy that all staff have signed up to and that it is available for young people.
- *Coherent team* – all practice members trained in being adolescent friendly.
- *Audit, evaluation and meaningful involvement of practice users* – using questionnaires to evaluate teenage services provided by the practice.
- *Health promotion* – ensuring that there is appropriate information provided for teenagers by leaflets, posters, consultations.
- *Accountability and performance* – acting on feedback from questionnaires.

- *Core requirements* – use 10 tips for how to make your practice teenage friendly (*see* Chapter 3).

Writing an action plan.

- *Agree who is involved* – identify team members and a person with ultimate responsibility for adolescent health.
- *Work out a timetable for the following:*
  - preliminary data gathering and completion of baseline by providers
  - development of a practice protocol for meeting young people's needs (*see* 10 tips in Chapter 3)
  - completion of staff training needs in the field of adolescent health
  - implementation of protocols by all staff members, e.g. confidentiality in practice leaflet
  - regular discussions of consultations with adolescents.

What additional resources will you require to execute your plan and from where do you hope to obtain them?

- Leaflets and posters from local health promotion unit, FPA, Brooks Advisory Clinic or designed by adolescents themselves.
- Training courses – check locally and nationally.
- Assess financial implications, e.g cost of training courses and who will pay.

Evaluating your learning plan. Re-audit in light of the 'action plan' above.

Disseminating the learning plan.

- Written protocols for all practice members.
- Regular reports on progress at practice meetings.
- Practice newsletter (if you have one).

Chapter 15

Remuneration for working with young people

Work with adolescents in general practice is remunerated as with all GP work, i.e. every patient registered receives a payment and this is augmented by claiming item of service payments. It is important for practices to have a system whereby all these items are claimed.

The following are some examples of payment claims.

GMS 3

These payments are for contraceptive advice to female patients, not for prescribing. Some health authorities provide practices with free condoms, but these are limited.

Immunisation

- Tetanus and polio 5 yearly
- Foreign travel
  - influenza
  - hepatitis B
  - pneumacoccal.

New patient registration

Some adolescents will wish to register as a new patient with a different partner from their family's GP. Some practices encourage all 16-year-olds to consider re-registering with the practice partner of their choice.

Temporary residence and emergency treatment

Young people often need medical treatment during their holidays when they are away from home.

Practices that are known to be teenage-friendly may attract these payments. Some practices are unwilling, for ethical reasons, to provide contraception services to under 16-year-olds. A practice can make it known that these patients are welcome. The practice can be paid through a temporary resident contraception claim on GMS 4/Section 36.

Local development scheme for GPs

These grants, known colloquially as LDS aim to improve the provision of primary care services. Practices need to submit proposals to their primary care group or trust or their local area health authority. Examples might be setting up a new adolescent clinic in the practice or a scheme by which adolescents are given birthday appointments to see the practice nurse for health promotion.

These payments must not duplicate existing arrangements but can be used to augment the infra-structure, i.e. the staff premises or computers.

PMS – pilots

Local authorities provide these as incentives to practices to provide services. Amongst such applications might be one to encourage improved access to medical care for adolescents. Again practices need to submit proposals to their local health authority, primary care groups/trusts for consideration.

For further details about remuneration for practices that provide increased services for adolescents make enquiries at your local level primary care group/trust or health authority.

Chapter 16

Questions for young people

This chapter includes questions aimed at young people that can be used by members of the practice team in a wide variety of ways.

- Displays on boards, etc.
- Handouts for the practice.
- Written questions aimed directly at teenagers coming to the practice.
- By GPs going into schools.
- Adolescent clinics.
- Auditing some aspects of the practice's practice.

A quiz

How old are you?

- 11–12.
- 13–14.
- 15–16.
- Over 16.

Are you:

- a boy?
- a girl?

You've been on holiday in Spain. You got bitten by loads of mosquitoes every night – scratch, scratch, scratch. What are the chances of you developing malaria now you're back?

- One in a thousand.
- One in a hundred.
- No chance at all.

You've been on holiday in Ibiza. You had unprotected sex with someone of the opposite sex. It was the time in the middle of her/your two periods. What are the chances that she/you got pregnant?

- One in ten.
- One in three.
- One in one (e.g. absolutely certain she/you will be pregnant!).

You've been on holiday in Brighton (welcome to the real world). You definitely didn't have AIDs when you went on holiday. You had unprotected sex with someone who has AIDs. What are the chances that you have come back from your holidays with AIDs?

- One in ten.
- One in a hundred.
- One in a thousand.

You have sex and help, help, help the condom bursts, falls off, gets lost or you haven't even used one! How long is there for you to get your emergency contraception pills into your mouth before they won't work any more?

- One day (24 hours).
- Three days (72 hours).

- Five days (120 hours).

OK – so do you know where to get the emergency contraceptive pills?

- Your own family doctor or any family doctor.
- Your local family planning or young people's clinic.
- Over the counter at your local chemist if you are over 15.
- All of these.

How often can you use emergency contraception?

- Once in a lifetime.
- Once a year.
- More than once a year.

How (un)fit are you? First take your pulse (count how many heart-beats in 30 seconds). Now, get a stopwatch and get ready … run hard on the spot for three minutes and then take your pulse again. Take your pulse again one minute later, and keep taking it every minute until it goes back to normal. How long did it take for your pulse to go back to what it was before?

- Less than one minute.
- One to three minutes.
- More than three minutes.

How many press-ups can you do in three minutes? (Make sure you bend your arms, not your back!).

- 0–14.
- 15–25.
- Over 26.

How many times can you step on and off a chair (make sure it's a strong chair) in three minutes?

- 0–20.

- 20–40.
- Over 40.

Can you put your hands flat on the ground with your knees straight?

- Yes.
- No.

Can you walk up and down the stairs in your house three times and then talk without being out of breath?

- Yes.
- No.

Is a standard unit of alcohol contained in:

- a glass of wine?
- a pint of beer?
- a measure of whisky?
- all of the above?

How many units of alcohol is it wise for a man not to exceed in any one week when drinking?

- 14 units.
- 21 units.
- 28 units.
- 35 units.
- 42 units.

How many units of alcohol is it wise for a woman not to exceed in any one week when drinking?

- 14 units.
- 21 units.
- 28 units.

- 35 units.
- 42 units.

How many times have you got drunk in the last four weeks?

- Not at all.
- One to three times.
- Four to seven times.
- More than seven times.

Do you think that your doctor will tell your parents things that you tell him/her?

- Yes.
- No.

Do you think your doctor is 'teenage friendly'?

- Yes.
- No.

Would you rather see a different doctor than the one who normally sees your parents?

- Yes.
- No.

When did you last go and see your doctor?

- Within the last week.
- More than one week ago but within the last three months.
- More than three months ago.

Is your family doctor:

- a man?
- a woman?

If you could choose, would you like your doctor to be:

- a man?
- a woman?

Chapter 17

Mental health in adolescents

Mental health problems in adolescents are often difficult to diagnose in primary care. Reasons for this include the following.

- Mood swings at this age are difficult to differentiate from the start of a psychiatric illness.
- Many young patients, especially young men, find it hard to describe their inner feelings.
- Emotional distress is frequently presented as a physical problem.
- Professionals and parents are reluctant to pin a psychiatric diagnosis on a young person.

Kramner and Garralda found that in one practice, after interviewing adolescents, 38% had 'psychiatric problems' while the practice records showed that GPs had only identified 12%.[1]

Looking back on the same practice's response to young men prior to their committing suicide also illustrates how difficult it is to identify distress in young people. One mother of a suicide son claimed 'GPs are often a stumbling block and people can't get beyond them – they are either not picking up, or they are rejecting what they are told'.

There is therefore a need for:

- awareness of the difficulties around early recognition and the need to learn from feedback from young people who have suffered from mental health conditions

- more discussion within the primary care team about difficulties encountered
- increased research and education about how mental illness presents in primary care.

In this chapter we touch on two functions that need to be performed by the primary care team.

1   Promoting emotional and mental health in young people.

2   Recognising and treating psychiatric problems.

Promoting mental health

This can be done whilst undertaking routine clinical practice by:

- conveying to every young person seen that they are valued by the practice. Much that is mentioned in this book helps to achieve this, i.e. making the practice team teenage-friendly, providing relevant information to young people, training staff and treating adolescents as competent individuals who require attention and explanations, and who should be allowed to make choices
- being aware of those adolescents who are facing extra stresses in their lives and taking action to support them when necessary. Examples include parents splitting up, serious illness or death in the family, not getting on at school, coping with chronic medical conditions
- communicating in a way that is appropriate to this age group (*see* Chapter 6).

Recognising psychiatric conditions

Depression

The high suicide rate amongst young men and self-harm amongst young women emphasise the importance of recognising depression before a crisis occurs. This is not easy. Depression hits young people in different ways. There appear to be three levels.

1 Intense mood swings which can be very profound and vary from day to day.

2 A syndrome of depressive symptoms including loss of energy, poor sleep, lack of concentration, reduced appetite, poor self-esteem and suicidal thoughts. This syndrome can last up to two weeks.

3 The above symptoms lasting more than two weeks becoming deeper and more chronic. When this occurs a serious depressive disorder should be considered.

Diagnosis is made difficult by the fact that these different levels are often presented by young people as a physical problem, i.e. headaches, fatigue, sore throat. When presented by a parent, they are more often presented as a conduct disorder, i.e. behaviour problems.

Questions that can be helpful in eliciting depression include:

• have you been feeling more 'down in the dumps', moody or tearful than usual?

• do these feelings last a short time or go on continuously?

• do such feelings interfere with your schoolwork, friendships or relationships at home?

Some physicians like to ask questions covering the different areas in the life of a young person using the acronym HEADS:

Home, Education, Activity, Drugs, Sex and Suicide

Other physicians find it helpful to use McWhinney's triple clinical approach, asking questions in the following areas:[2]

Biochemical: manic depressive illness in the family.

Individual: psychological and emotional problems in the past.

Social: bullying, trouble with relationships, death of someone close, etc.

Whichever way the emotional state of the patient is solicited, the primary care worker needs to provide sufficient time for the adolescent to describe in his or her own words the feelings they are experiencing. It is essential to interview the patient alone and to acquire some collateral information from parents, school, etc.

Management of depression

The following are worth considering.

- Empathy and active listening by a caring physician or a friend can be therapeutic. It is therefore helpful to encourage young people to choose a member of the primary care team and/or a friend in which to confide.

- Encourage depressed adolescents to do something each day that they used to enjoy, i.e. see a friend, play favourite music, go for a swim, and pat themselves on the back when they have done it.

- The physicians should likewise congratulate any depressed adolescents for coming to the practice and sharing their feelings.

- It is always worth emphasising that these depressive feelings tend to shift in this age group in a week or two but if they continue over two weeks it is important to return for treatment, which could be:
  - medication
  - referral
  - further support.

When it comes to medication, research shows that tricyclates are not effective in this age group and also run the risk of being used in suicide. Selected Serotonin Reuptake Inhibitors are better tolerated and probably more effective. However, there are no trials to confirm this.

When it comes to referrals it is important for the practice to know what is available locally and how long their waiting time is likely to be. Services vary widely in their availability and responsiveness. It can also be helpful to have a list of charitable services which can be contacted by the patient if required in the meantime (*see* box below).

Samaritans: 08457 909090
www.samaritans.org.uk

Childline: 0800 1111
www.childline.org.uk

Saneline: 0845 767 8000
www.sane.org.uk

Depression Alliance: 0207 633 0557
www.depressionalliance.org

Conduct disorders

Antisocial behaviour is one of the most common reasons for referral of adolescent patients. There is research showing much co-morbidity between depression and conduct disorders. There is also an association between anti-social behaviour, depression and substance misuse.[3] Attention deficit hyperactivity disorder (ADHD) and conduct disorders are also associated.

Aggressive parenting and lack of parental supervision have been shown to aggravate the condition but conduct disorders can also drive parents to emotionally withdraw and become more aggressive towards their teenage children.

Meta-analysis shows that the more TV violence that is seen the more aggressive young people tend to be.

Assessment

Parents and patients need to be interviewed separately and then possibly together. It is also helpful to interview school staff and relevant others.

Interventions

Much has been written about different interventions and their evaluation – these cover educational, social, legal and community interventions. All these claim to ameliorate anti-social behaviour.

Psychosomatic disorders

Anxiety and depression are at the root of many of these conditions,[4] but there are other stresses in an adolescent life that can lead to this condition – peer group problems, academic pressure perhaps associated with learning difficulties, and family disruption. Temperament plays a part, for example an obsessional trait leading to perfectionism in a high achiever puts enormous self-imposed pressure on an adolescent.

Parental reaction is also important, parental belief and temperament all play a part, as does the family's ability to communicate painful and angry feelings.

Treatment

It is essential to eliminate a physical condition. However, there must be a limit placed on the number of tests undertaken. Once the physician is convinced that this is a psychosomatic disorder then gradual rehabilitative endeavours need to be encouraged with some face saving activity like physiotherapy or relaxation classes. It can also be beneficial to work with parents, encouraging them to accept that no further physical investigations are required and to accept that the need for rehabilitation services and the expression of distressed feelings within the family, both verbally and non-verbally, will help.

More research is needed into what treatments are most effective.

Psychotic disorders

Early recognition is important in this distressing illness in order to reduce both the immediate suffering of the patient and long-term morbidity. Sadly, many episodes of first onset psychosis go unrecognised by the primary care teams.

Once the diagnosis is suspected it is important to build a positive relationship with the patient so that further assessment and treatment can take place, probably in tier 2 mental services. If such a relationship cannot be achieved and the young person, or others to whom they are aggressive, is at risk of injury, consideration has to be given to sectioning the patient. It is therefore important that all members of the primary care team know the rulings of the Mental Health Act (or equivalent in Wales or Scotland) and that they develop a good working relationship with their local psychiatric services and social workers on call for emergencies.

It is important for physicians to differentiate between the early stages of a psychotic illness and a psychotic attack brought on by substance misuse (*see* substance abuse below). The following may be of help.

- Biochemically induced psychosis will vanish after a few days if the patient abstains from substance misuse.

- A schizophrenic has usually had difficulties in their past personal relationships.

- Accurate history taking and strict adherence to diagnostic criteria usually differentiate between these two conditions helped by referral to second tier services.

Maintenance treatment

Primary care teams play a significant part in helping to maintain the treatment of the few, but important, schizophrenics on their list and in helping them to maximise their functioning. In these days of rotas and weekend holidays all members of the team should know about these vulnerable patients and if possible build some sort of relationship with them so that they are prepared if they are on call and a patient needs to be dealt with as an emergency.

Substance abuse

Substance abuse is a confusing term and is best replaced with 'substance misuse' or simply 'substance use' meaning the non-medical use of chemical substances in order to achieve alterations in psychological functioning. Substances include alcohol, nicotine, illegal drugs and prescribed drugs, as well as volatile substances.

Drug use can be divided into:

- experimental

- recreational, i.e. continued after initial experiment

- dependent, i.e. compulsion to continue in order to avoid abstinence symptoms or for further psychic benefits, which can be divided into either physical or psychological dependence.

In adolescents, substance misuse is less likely to require medical treatment for dependence and most likely to be a symptom of behaviour or conduct disorder, or a method of numbing depression.

A survey of 15 000 15/16-year-old Europeans found British school children had the highest prevalence for drug taking – 42% – with Ireland second at 37% and the Czech Republic at 23%. More worrying was that the British lead in taking a drug ten times or more (22% of UK school children) with the Italians coming in second at 9%.

Risk factors

Alcohol intake and smoking, especially amongst women, is also high in the UK. These are similar to the risk factors for behavioural disorders, as are the protective factors.

In a survey of adolescents referred to psychiatric units after detoxification, 42% had conduct disorders, 35% major depression, 21% a mixture of attention deficit, hypersensitivity and impulsive disorder.

Substance misuse can be a significant factor in self-harm and suicide. One third of adolescents who harm themselves are intoxicated – while alcohol and unsafe sex are closely related.

Identification

Most adolescents will keep their drug use a secret. Criminal activity to fund the habit can lead to prosecution, as can accidents whilst under the influence. History taking can be aided by urine analysis (heroin, cocaine and amphetamines may not be revealed after 48 hours). Breath Alcohol Meters are also useful – a high reading without intoxication indicates tolerance. Chronic alcohol intake asks for liver function tests and the use of dirty needles can indicate a need to test for HIV and Hep. C.

Treatment

If you are seriously concerned about a young person who is abusing drugs then it is best to liaise with the local services specialising in substance misuse treatments. The practice team can also help by continuing to see their patient to monitor their progress and to refer for psychiatric help where this is indicated.

Eating disorders in young people

Many young people, more girls than boys, will have some type of eating disorder during their teens, but most of these will not be severe enough to fall under the heading of 'eating disorders'. Even the milder cases of 'actual' eating disorders resolve without any formal treatment or acknowledgement that there is, or has been, a problem.

It is, however, quite difficult to be able to differentiate between 'chaotic eating' and 'anorexia and/or bulimia'. Bulimia is more common than anorexia and tends to occur in older teenagers. One in three girls with bulimia will have also had a history of anorexia. As the outcome of anorexia is so much more serious than that of bulimia, the details of the identification and management of the problem are given below.

The outcome of anorexia is that five out of ten recover, three out of ten improve without being completely cured and may subsequently develop bulimia, and two out of ten carry on having severe problems.

Cognitive therapy is the best management for bulimia. Self-help is effective and should be encouraged in the first instance. *Overcoming Binge Eating* by CG Fairburn can be strongly recommended for individuals to read.[5]

Case study of a teenager with anorexia nervosa

Mrs B brings her 16-year-old daughter, Polly, to see you, worried that she has an eating disorder. Polly is reluctant to see the doctor, denying that she has a problem. Mother says that Polly has been on a strict diet for the last six months and has lost two stone in weight – she now weighs six stone and her periods have stopped. She is obviously very thin.

What issues you should cover.

- Take a careful history: the diagnosis of anorexia nervosa is made from the history and mental state examination; there are no specific tests or investigations to confirm the diagnosis.

- You need to check her height and weight to calculate the BMI (*see* Appendix). A rapid rate of weight loss (more that 1 kg per week) as well as very low weight (BMI less than 15) are causes for concern.

- If she is abusing laxatives/diuretics or vomiting frequently she may have electrolyte imbalance (hypokalamemia is the most common abnormality) and this can, although rarely, lead to cardiac arrythmias and sudden death.

- Assess co-existent psychopathology, particularly depression, as there is an increased risk of suicide in this group of patients.

- Blood tests do not contribute directly to the diagnosis but a baseline screen (FBC, U&Es and blood glucose) is appropriate.

- An ECG should be performed if the BMI is less than 15 as this sometimes shows abnormalities indicating an increased risk of cardiac arrythmias: prolongation of the QT interval is an indication for cardiological referral.

- Consider bone densitometry in women with amenorrhoea of over six months duration. Osteoporosis is a common and potentially serious consequence of anorexia nervosa and is resistant to drug and hormonal treatments.

- In most cases of anorexia nervosa, early specialist referral is indicated as treatment is time-consuming and often difficult.

What you should do.

- Ask to see Polly alone at first to build a rapport with her and hear things from her perspective. At the end of the consultation you could speak to her mother again, with Polly's permission.

- Ask about her eating habits – in anorexia nervosa her diet will be highly restrictive with avoidance of all 'fattening' foods.

- Patients with anorexia nervosa also exhibit a characteristic set of attitudes to shape and weight with a 'morbid fear of fatness' and 'relentless pursuit of thinness'.

- She may exercise excessively, vomit after eating or abuse laxatives/diuretics. Some will also binge.

- Ask about depression and anxiety symptoms. These are common in anorexia nervosa and can be very distressing, as are obsessional and compulsive features.

- Family relationships are often strained, especially around meal times, and the patient usually becomes withdrawn socially and may feel isolated.

- She may be troubled by a variety of physical symptoms, including feeling cold all the time, loss of concentration, tiredness, dizziness, muscle weakness, peripheral oedema, constipation, dry skin – these are all physical effects of starvation.

- Once you have established the diagnosis, you need to help Polly to accept that she has a significant illness. This may take time and you should initially arrange to see her weekly for support and monitoring. If she is prepared to see a specialist you should refer her without delay.

- In milder cases (teenagers with eating disorder of six months duration or less and BMI over 15) it may be reasonable to offer an initial trial of treatment in general practice. This involves a combination of common sense nutritional advice, emotional support and careful monitoring of weight to ensure weight gain. Parents and sometimes siblings should be involved and are likely to need considerable support from the GP.

Diagnostic criteria for anorexia nervosa.

1 Characteristic over-evaluation of shape and weight with intense fear of becoming fat.

2 Active maintenance of an unduly low weight (BMI of less than 17.5) achieved mainly by strict dieting and excessive exercising and, in a minority, self-induced vomiting.

3 Amenorrhoea for at least three months (if not on the contraceptive Pill).

Conclusions

Although many of the conditions discussed in this section can appear difficult to handle, there is much those working in a primary care team can do to make a significant difference to the young people presenting with them. It is worth remembering that:

- listening and giving time can be therapeutic
- building bridges to others who can help is often the best thing one can do
- extra training is possible and can provide extra confidence
- sharing difficult mental health problems with a colleague, the whole team or a psychiatrist can be supportive.

There are many other conditions which require skill, time and possibly outside help before those working in primary care can elicit and treat the mental and emotional problems that cause or result from difficulties encountered by adolescents.

These conditions include:

- physical or sexual abuse
- being excluded from school
- taking an overdose – or other forms of self-harm
- having a serious chronic or life-threatening medical condition
- being in or just leaving 'care'
- being a schoolgirl mother.

References

1 Kramner T and Garralda M (1996) Psychiatric disorders in adolescents in primary care. *Br J Psych.* **173:** 508–13.

2 McWhinney I (1996) *A Textbook of Family Medicine.* Oxford University Press, Oxford.

3 Windle M (1990) A longitudinal study of antisocial behaviors in early adolescence as predictors of late adolescent substance use: gender and ethnic group differences. *J Abnorm Psychol.* **99:** 86–91.

4 Garralda M (1996) Somatisation in children. *J Child Psychol Psychiatr.* **37:** 13–33.

5 Fairburn CG (1995) *Overcoming Binge Eating.* Guildford Press, New York.

Chapter 18

Example of a practice leaflet for adolescents

Statement you might include in your general practice leaflet

This practice welcomes teenagers. We offer a confidential service which means we will not divulge any information you give us (except in exceptional circumstances). We will provide contraception, including emergency contraception, whatever your age, and the doctors will not discuss this with your parents. The doctors and nurses are all trained in contraception.

A PRACTICE GUIDE FOR ADOLESCENTS

Some useful medical details about you

Name ....

NHS No. ....

Date ....

Your blood pressure ....

Your height ....

Your weight ....

Immunisations:

Measles	Yes/No
Rubella	Yes/No
MMR (measles, mumps and rubella)	Yes/No
Polio	Yes/No
Meningococcal	Yes/No

The 'little' medical guide

Headaches

Everyone gets headaches from time to time. If you develop a very severe headache or it is associated with a high fever, a stiff neck or a rash, it could be meningitis, so contact us quickly.

Coughs, colds and flu-like illnesses

Most of these are caused by viruses and cannot be treated with antibiotics. There are, however, a number of things you can do to relieve the unpleasant symptoms of:

- sore throat
- aching limbs
- headache
- fevers.

Take lots of fluids and regular soluble aspirin or paracetamol. Gargling helps a very sore throat. You will usually begin to feel better after a few days. If it does not settle or you begin to feel worse, you can contact your college sister or the doctor.

If you have a sore throat which lasts longer than expected, it is possible that you have glandular fever. There is a blood test available to check the diagnosis. Usually there is no specific treatment and the advice is much the same as for other viruses.

Diarrhoea and vomiting
This can be unpleasant but does not usually last long. If you are being sick, take small regular sips of water – you will absorb some and it helps stop dehydration. A hot water bottle can help to relieve stomach ache. Vomiting usually stops within a few hours but diarrhoea can last longer. This can be helped by not eating but drinking lots of clear fluids for 24 hours. Avoid milk during this time. If you have just come back from exotic places it is worth coming to see the doctor to get it checked out.

Emergencies

Ring the practice if you are faced with an emergency as most emergencies can be dealt with by the practice doctor.

You can contact a practice doctor for urgent consultations and visits 24 hours a day, 7 days a week.

Telephone: ....

Out of working hours there will be a recorded message giving you an emergency number to ring.

Confidentiality

You can be absolutely sure that anything you discuss with any member of the practice team (family doctor, nurses, receptionists, etc.) will stay absolutely confidential and nothing will be said to anyone (parents, etc.) without your permission.

Clinics that we run

You can discuss any health problem with any doctor at any time, but we also run specialist clinics.

These include:

- a travel clinic
- a contraception clinic
- an asthma clinic
- a drop in teenage clinic.

**Include individual details for your practice.

There is an Accident and Emergency service at the

....

hospital in

....

Telephone: ....

And an eye casualty department at the eye hospital.

Complaints

The practice has a comments, complaints and suggestions procedure, details of which are available in the waiting rooms or at reception.

Contraception

All the doctors and nurses are trained in all the different methods of contraception.

You can get advice in the special contra-ception clinics or any routine surgery.

Abortion

We believe that women should have the opportunity to have an abortion if they wish. All the doctors are happy to advise and help. Other sources of help and information include:

**Include other organisations.

Emergency contraception

Have you:

- taken a risk?
- forgotten your Pill?
- burst a condom?

You have 72 hours (3 days) in which to act – BUT the sooner the better!

Help is also available from:

**Include clinics.

(An emergency coil can also be fitted up to five days after unprotected intercourse).

Counselling

Are you suffering from stress, exam problems, sexual problems, eating disorders (anorexia and bulimia), loneliness, depression?

The places to get help include the practice – all the doctors are happy to see you with these types of problems; we offer individual and group anxiety management, a programme for help with bulimia and yoga classes.

Chapter 19

Resources for teenage health

Websites for teenagers

- www.teenagehealthfreak.org
- www.doctorann.org
- www.youthhealth.com
- www.Brook.org.uk
- www.lovelife.uk.com
- www.lifebytes.gov.uk
- www.ruthinking.co.uk

General books for teenagers

- Macfarlane A and McPherson A (2002) *Diary of a Teenage Health Freak* (3e). Oxford University Press, Oxford.
- McPherson A and Macfarlane A (2002) *Diary of the Other Health Freak* (3e). Oxford University Press, Oxford.

Books for parents

- Macfarlane A and McPherson A (1999) *Teenagers: the agony, the ecstasy, the answers*. Little Brown, London.
- Palmer RL (1989) *Anorexia – a guide for sufferers and their families*. Penguin, Harmondsworth.
- Fairburn CG (1995) *Overcoming Binge Eating*. Guildford Press, New York.

Videos for professionals

Clueless and *Trust* are both videos concerning teenagers in contact with the primary healthcare services. They are ten minutes long and can be used in general practice for training purposes. Each shows four interviews with a young person in a surgery and is designed to encourage discussion on how to improve primary healthcare services for young people. They are available for £7.00 each from the Royal College of General Practitioners, 14 Princes Gate, London SW7 1PU. Tel: 020 7581 3232; email: sales@rcgp.org.uk.

Website for those interested in training in adolescent health

www.euteach.com = European Training in Effective Adolescent Care and Health.

This site has been developed by a consortium of international adolescent health experts. The curriculum is divided into 17 modules – 8 general and 9 specific.

The general modules are as follows.

1 Definition of adolescence.

2 Overview of adolescent health, epidemiology and priorities.

3 Family, influences and dynamics.

4 Setting, communication and clinical skills.

5 Confidentiality, consent and access.

6 Context and impact, socio-economic, cultural, ethnic and gender issues.

7 Resources, resilience, exploratory and risk behaviours.

8 Health education and health promotion, including school health.

The specific modules are as follows.

1 Growth and puberty.

2 Nutrition, exercise and obesity.

3 Sexual and reproductive health.

4 Common medical conditions of adolescence.

5 Chronic conditions.

6 Mental health.

7 Eating disorders.

8 Substance use and misuse.

9 Injuries and violence, including accidents, self-harm, abuse, etc.

Other adolescent health teaching resources for the primary care team, undergraduates and CME

- *Confidentiality Toolkit* – available free from the Royal College of General Practitioners, 14 Princes Gate, London SW7 1PU. Tel: 020 7581 3232; email: sales@rcgp.org.uk.

- Book and video by T Hughes, ME Garralda and A Tylee. *Child Mental Health Problems: a booklet on child psychiatric problems for General Practitioners.* Available from the Department of Child and Adolescent Pyschiatry, Paddington Green, London W2 1LQ. Tel: 020 7886 1145.

- *Key Data on Adolescence 2001* by John Coleman and Jane Schofield. Available from the Trust for the Study of Adolescence, 23 New Road, Brighton, East Sussex, BN1 1WZ. Tel: 01273 693311; email: info@tsa.uk.com; website: www.tsa.uk.com. Excellent data source which is updated every two years and contains a large number of tables covering key data including population; family and households; children and young people in care/looked after; education and training; employment; physical health; sexual health; mental health; crime. **This organisation also provides excellent information, literature and training courses.**

Useful organisations

Listed here are voluntary organisations, agencies and support services that can offer help and information on a wide range of subjects to both parents and young people.

Index to topics

Alcohol | Bereavement | Bullying | Counselling and mental health | Drugs | Eating disorders | Family and young people | Gambling | Health | HIV/AIDS | Legal rights | Parenting | Sexual health | Sexual assault | Sexuality | Smoking | Special needs | Suicidal feelings.

Alcohol

- **Accept**
  724 Fulham Road
  London
  SW6 5SE
  Tel: 020 7371 7477

Organisation to support and advise those with drink problems and their families.

- **Alcoholics Anonymous**
  Tel: 020 7833 0022 (10am–10pm, 365 days a year)
  National Helpline: 0845 7697 555

  Organisation to help alcoholics achieve sobriety and stay sober. Meetings held locally.

- **Drinkline**
  National Alcohol Helpline: 0800 917 8282 (9am–11pm, Mon–Fri; 6pm–11pm, Sat–Sun)

- **National Association for Children of Alcoholics**
  Helpline: 0800 289 061

Bereavement

- **CRUSE – Bereavement Care**
  Cruse House
  126 Sheen Road
  Richmond
  Surrey
  TW9 1UR
  Tel: 020 8940 4818
  Bereavement line: 0845 758 5565

- **Compassionate Friends**
  53 North Street
  Bristol
  BS3 1EN
  Tel: 0117 966 5202
  Helpline: 0117 953 9639

  A nationwide self-help organisation of parents whose child (of any age including adult) has died from any cause.

Bullying

- **Anti-bullying Campaign**
  185 Tower Bridge Road
  London
  SE1 2UF
  Tel: 020 7378 1446

  Helps parents on how to work with schools to combat the problem
  of bullying. Gives telephone advice to parents and children.

Counselling and mental health

- **British Association for Counselling**
  1 Regent Place
  Rugby
  Warwickshire
  CB21 2PJ
  Tel: 0870 4435252

  For information and advice on practising counsellors and
  organisations in your area.

- **Institute of Family Therapy**
  24–32 Stephenson Way
  London
  NW1 2HX
  Tel: 020 7391 9150

  Offers a clinical service to families who are experiencing psychological, behavioural or relationship problems, including those
  centred on children or adolescents. Problems are viewed in a
  family context and families are helped to find their own solutions.

- **Mental Health Foundation**
  7th Floor
  83 Victoria Street
  London
  SW1H OHW
  Tel: 020 7802 0300

- **Relate: National Marriage Guidance**
  Herbert Gray College
  Little Church Street
  Rugby
  Warwickshire
  CV21 3AP
  Tel: 01788 573241

  Co-ordinates about 160 local Relate centres which offer education in personal relationships as well as providing counselling for people seeking help in marriage and family relationships.

- **The Samaritans**
  Helpline: 08457 909090

  Offer a 24-hour confidential telephone helpline for people who are in despair and who feel suicidal.

- **Young Minds**
  The National Association for Child and Family Mental Health
  102–108 Clerkenwell Road
  London
  EC1M 5SA
  Tel: 020 7336 8445
  Parents' Information Service: 0800 018 2138

  Young Minds aims to raise awareness about the emotional and behavioural problems of children and young people, and to inform the public about the more common problems and the help that is available.

- **Youth Access**
  2 Taylor's Yard
  67 Alderbrook Road
  London
  SW12 8AD
  Tel: 020 8772 9900 (9.30am–4.30pm, Mon–Fri)

  Provides addresses of the nearest counselling and advice centres for young people.

Drugs

- **ADFAM**
  Waterbridge House
  32–36 Loman Street
  London
  SE1 0EE
  Tel: 020 7928 8898
  Helpline: 020 7928 8900

  Offers information and confidential support to families of drug users. Runs a national telephone helpline.

- **Crimestopper SNAP – Say No And Phone Campaign**
  Tel: 0800 555111 (free call)

  SNAP is the nationwide Crimestoppers campaign aimed at tackling the drug problem. You can call anonymously (you won't be asked your name, address, or 'phone number) if you know anyone who regularly supplies drugs or who commits any crime.

- **Drug Scope**
  32–36 Loman Street
  London
  SE1 OEE
  Tel: 020 7928 1211

- **National Drugs Helpline**
  Tel: 0800 776600

  A free 24-hour, 365 days a year confidential service available in English and other languages. The helpline gives information, advice and counselling, offering constructive and supportive referrals and literature to callers with concerns about drugs and solvents.

- **Release**
  388 Old Street
  London
  EC1V 9LT
  Advice line: 020 7729 9904 (10am–6pm, Mon–Fri)
  24-hour emergency line: 020 7603 8654

  Confidential service for drug-related legal problems. Concerned with the welfare of users (of both illegal and prescribed drugs) and their family and friends. Offers emergency help in cases of arrest.

Eating disorders

- **Eating Disorders Association**
  First Floor
  Wensume House
  103 Prince of Wales Road
  Norwich
  NR1 1DW

  Youth Helpline for those aged 18 years and younger: 01603 765 050 (4pm–6pm, Mon–Fri)

  General Helpline: 01603 621414
  Youth Helpline: 01603 765050

  Aims to help and support all those affected by anorexia and bulimia nervosa, especially sufferers, the families of sufferers and other carers.

Family and young people

- **British Agencies for Adoption and Fostering (BAAF)**
  Skyline House
  200 Union Street
  London
  SE1 0LX
  Tel: 020 7593 2000

Aims to promote the highest standards of practice in adoption, fostering and social work with children and families. Contact BAAF to find out which adoption agencies cover the area where you live.

- **Centre for Fun and Families**
  12 Upperton Road
  Leicester
  LE3 OBG
  Tel: 0116 2234254

  The centre runs parallel groups for parents and teenagers and offers training to staff running parenting programmes.

- **Childline**
  Royal Mail Building
  Studd Street
  London
  NW1 0QW

  Freepost 1111
  London
  N1 OBR
  Tel: 020 7239 1000
  Helpline: 0800 1111 (24 hours a day, 365 days a year)

  Provides a national telephone helpline for children and young people in danger or distress who want to talk to a trained counsellor. All calls are free and confidential. Publishes leaflets and books for parents and professionals.

- **Children's Society (Church of England Children's Society)**
  Edward Rudolf House
  69–85 Margery Street
  London
  WC1X OJL
  Admin: 020 7841 4400
  Enquiries: 020 7841 4436

Runs various family centres and social projects, e.g. young parents group. Many of these provide information and advice, especially on financial matters. Produces publications and information packs, e.g. *Education for Parenthood* aimed at 15–18-year-olds in school.

- **Family and Youth Concern**
  322 Woodstock Road
  Oxford
  OX2 7NS
  Tel: 01865 351966

  Aims to preserve stable family life. Undertakes research into the effects of marital breakdown and public education programmes on family welfare and personal relationships. Information leaflets available on parenting.

- **Family Rights Group**
  The Print House
  18 Ashwin Street
  London
  E8 3DL
  Tel: 020 7923 2628
  Advice line: 0800 731 1696 (1.30pm–3.30pm, Mon–Fri)

  Provides advice and support for families whose children are involved with social services.

- **Gingerbread**
  7 Sovereign Close
  Sovereign Court
  London
  E1W 3HW
  Tel: 020 7488 9300

  Provides day-to-day support and practical help for lone parents and their children via a national network of local self-help groups. The national office also provides a phone advice service for lone parents.

- **National Children's Bureau**
  8 Wakley Street
  London
  EC1V 7QE
  Tel: 020 7843 6000

  A national inter-disciplinary association concerned with the needs of children and young people in the family, school and society. Undertakes research and policy and practice development. Provides a library and information service, seminars and training. Sister organisations:

  - **Children in Scotland**
    Princes House
    5 Shandwick Place
    Edinburgh
    EH2 4RG
    Tel: 0131 228 8484

  - **Children in Wales**
    25 Windsor Place
    Cardiff
    CF10 3BZ
    Tel: 029 2034 2434

- **National Council for One Parent Families**
  255 Kentish Town Road
  London
  NW5 2LX
  Tel: 020 7428 5400

  Runs an information service for lone parents. Provides re-employment training for lone parents and rights-based training for professionals working with lone parents.

- **National Foster Care Association**
  87 Blackfriar Road
  London
  SE1 8HA
  Tel: 020 7620 6400

  A national charity providing advice, information and training on issues relating to young people and foster care.

- **NSPCC**
  42 Curtain Road
  London
  EC2A 3NH
  Tel: 020 7825 2500
  Helpline: 0808 800 5000 (24 hours)

  Aims to prevent child abuse and neglect in all its forms, to give practical help to families with children at risk, and to encourage public awareness. Runs more than 80 child protection projects in England. Operates the free 24-hour National Child Protection Helpline.

Health

- **Changing Faces**
  1–2 Junction Mews
  London
  W2 1PN
  Tel: 020 7706 4232
  email: info@changingfaces.co.uk
  Web: www.changingfaces.co.uk

  The charity supports children and adults who have a disfigurement and it works with health and social care professionals.

- **NHS Direct**
  Tel: 0845 4647

HIV/AIDS

- **National AIDS Helpine**
  Tel: 0800 567123 (free and confidential) available 24 hours a
  day, 7 days a week.

  Questions or worries about AIDS can be discussed with a
  trained advisor.

Legal rights

- **Children's Legal Centre**
  University of Essex
  Wivenhoe Park
  Colchester
  Essex
  CO4 3SQ
  Tel: 01206 872466
  Advice line: 01206 873820

  For information and advice on any aspect of law and policy
  affecting children and young people.

Parenting

- **National Family and Parenting Institute**
  430 Highgate Studios
  53–79 Highgate Road
  Kentish Town
  London
  NW5 1TL
  Tel: 020 7424 3460

  The Institute has been established to provide families with
  support in undertaking parenting. Its functions include policy
  development, research and public education.

- **Parentline Plus**
  (Incorporates Parentline, the National Stepfamily Association and Parent Network.)
  Unit 520 Highgate Studios
  53–57 Highgate Road
  London
  NW5 1TL
  Tel: 020 72845500
  Helpline: 0808 8002222 (9am–9pm, Mon–Fri; 9.30am–5pm, Sat; 10am–3pm, Sun)
  Textphone for the hard of hearing: 0800 7836783
  email: headoffice@parentlineplus.org.uk

  Runs a Helpline and parenting courses for anyone in a parenting role and provides services to professionals dealing with young people and families.

Sexual health

- **Brook Advisory Service**
  421 Highgate Studios
  53–79 Highgate Road
  London
  NW5 1TL
  Tel: 020 7284 6040
  Brook Helpline: 020 7617 8000
  Young People's Helpline: 0800 0185 023

  Offers a counselling and advice service. Leaflets and posters available from 01865 719410.

- **Family Planning Association**
  2–12 Pentonville Road
  London
  N1 9FP
  Tel: 020 7837 5432
  Helpline: 020 7837 4044/0845 310 1334 (9am–7pm, Mon–Fri)

Offers information on all aspects of family planning and sexual health, including advice for parents on how to talk to their children about sexual matters – free leaflets available. They also operate a Helpline for anyone who wants information on contraception and sexual health.

Sexual assault

- **Rape Crisis Helplines**
  Look in the telephone directory or ring Directory Enquiries on 192 for the Helpline number in your area. Provide free confidential support and advice to victims of rape.

- **Survivors (Male Rape)**
  Tel: 020 7613 0808 (7pm–10pm, Mon and Wed)

Sexuality

- **FFLAG: Friends and Families of Lesbians and Gays**
  PO Box 84
  Exeter
  EX4 4AN
  Helplines: 01454 852418
  National Coordinator: 01392 279 546

- **Parents Helpline**
  PO Box 100
  15 Pritchard Street
  Manchester
  M1 7DA
  Tel: 0161 748 3452 (All lines open 10am–10pm, 7 days a week)

  A national organisation staffed by volunteers, offering confidential support for parents and their gay, lesbian and bi-sexual sons or daughters. Also provides information leaflets and other support contacts in the UK.

- **Lesbian and Gay Switchboard**
  Tel: 020 7837 7324 (24 hours a day)

  Offers information and advice to lesbians and gay men and their families and friends.

Smoking

- **Quit – The National Society for Non-smokers**
  211 Old Street
  London
  EC1V 9NR
  Tel: 020 7251 1551
  Quitline: 0800 002200 (staffed by qualified counsellors trained in helping smokers give up). Open 1pm–9pm.

  Quit produce literature, act as a source of information on quitting and conduct high profile publicity campaigns.

Special needs

- **Asian People with Disabilities Alliance (APDA)**
  The Disability Alliance Centre
  Central Middlesex Hospital
  The Old Refectory
  Acton Lane
  London
  NW10 7NS
  Tel: 020 8961 6778

  Aims to ensure that Asian people with disabilities are accorded full status, rights and facilities to enable them to participate fully and represent their own interests in all areas of society. Provides advice, support and respite day care services.

- **Contact a Family**
  209–211 City Road
  London
  EC1V 1JN
  Tel: 020 7608 8700

  Brings families whose children have disabilities together. Offers advice and guidance to parents who wish to start a support group whether in their neighbourhood or nationally through a network of local and national mutual support and self-help groups.

- **Council for Disabled Children**
  8 Wakley Street
  London
  EC1V 7QE
  Tel: 020 7843 6000

  As part of the National Children's Bureau, the Council for Disabled Children aims to promote cooperation between different professional, voluntary, and statutory organisations concerned with children and young people with disabilities and their families. They have produced a guide for parents of children with special needs called 'Help Starts Here'.

Suicidal feelings

- **The Samaritans**
  Helpline: 08457 909090

  Offer a 24-hour confidential telephone and email helpline for people who are in despair and who feel suicidal. There are more than 23 000 volunteers nationwide.

Other resources that are useful in adolescent health

At What Age Can I? An updated edition of the Children's Legal Centre's comprehensive guide to age-based legislation affecting children and young people.	C Hamilton	The Children's Legal Centre, Essex Tel: 01206 873820
Coping with Young Children A practical handbook for professionals wishing to work with parents who are experiencing severe difficulties with their children.	J Duguay and P Pritchard	Jillian Duguay Tel: 01685 810323 Pam Pritchard Tel: 01443 443383
Developing Parenting Programmes Describes content, methods and materials of the range of parenting programmes available.	C Smith	National Children's Bureau Enterprises, London Tel: 020 7843 6000
Helping Children with Ill or Disabled Parents *A guide for parents and professionals* Looks at the range of issues that can arise and suggests positive ways in which these can be approached.	J Segal and J Simkins	Jessica Kingsley Publishers, London
Is it Legal? A parents' guide to the law Information on how the law affects the day-to-day lives of parents and families.	G Keep and C Hamilton	National Family and Parenting Institute, London Tel: 020 7424 3460

Parenting a Young Child with Conduct Problems A qualitative research of parents living with conduct-problem children.	C Webster-Stratton and A Spitzer	Advances in Clinical Child Psychology, Vol. 18 ed. by TH Ollendick and RJ Prinz. Plenum Press, New York, 1996
Parenting: what really counts? The book examines the scientific evidence on what really matters for children's healthy psychological development.	S Golombok	Routledge, London
Supporting Parents of Teenagers: A handbook for professionals. Provides a review of current policy developments and addresses the practical issues of how to assess and provide support for parents.	Edited by Dr J Coleman and Dr D Roker	Jessica Kingsley Publishers, London
Teenagers: A survival guide for parents Video and booklet Looks at common sources of friction between parents and teenagers such as coming home late, peer pressure, stress, drugs and sex.	Dr J Coleman and Carlton TV	Carlton TV, PO Box 11, London WC2N 4AW
Teenagers in the Family Skills for parents. Designed to assist in understanding teenage behaviour and development.	Dr J Coleman	Trust for the Study of Adolescence, Brighton Tel: 01273 693311

Appendix

Percentile charts of height, weight, BMI, and stages of pubertal changes

Amongst the health problems associated with adolescence are those relating to growth, the growth spurt, obesity and body changes which take place during puberty. Adolescents and their parents are frequently concerned with what the normal range of height, weight and pubertal changes are at different ages.

The percentile charts giving the normal range of development at different ages are therefore included in the next few pages for reference.

Full instructions on the use of these percentile charts and copies of the charts for use by individuals can be obtained from Harlow Printing Limited, Maxwell Street, South Shields, Tyne & Wear, NE33 4PU; tel: 0191 455 4286; fax: 0191 420 0195; email: sales@ harlowprinting.co.uk.

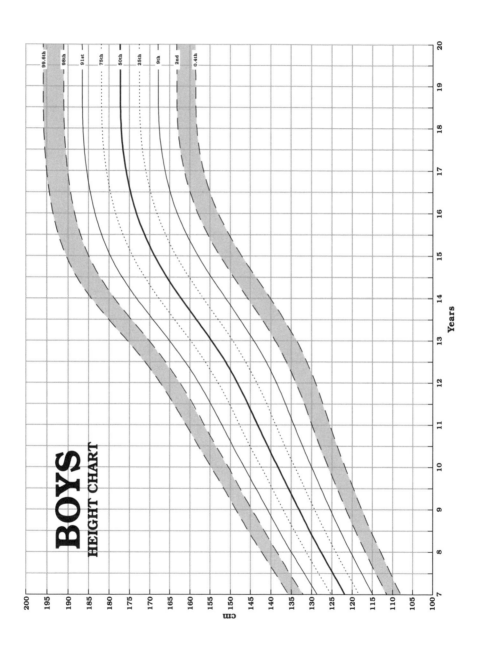

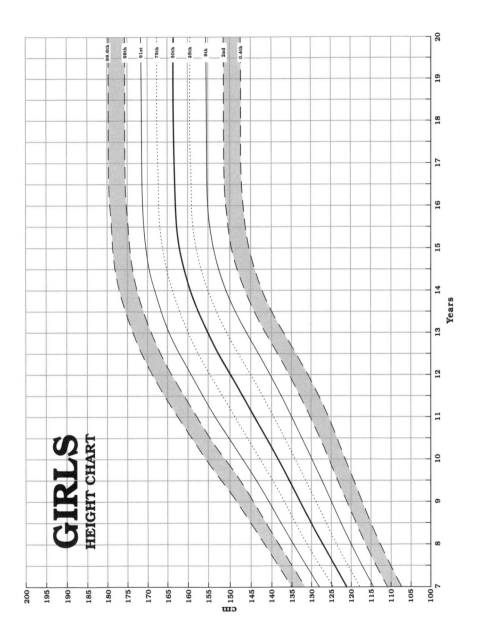

GIRLS
HEIGHT CHART

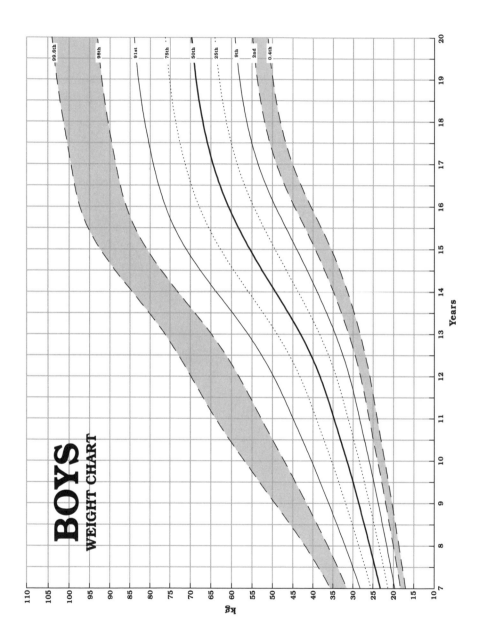

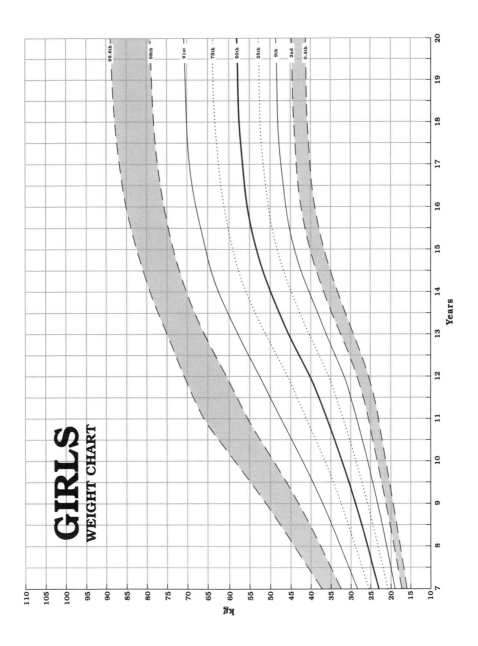

Because a high BMI by itself may not be a guarantor of obesity/overweight, a high waist centile added to a high BMI centile will confirm fatness more conclusively.

Measuring the waist

The waist is defined as the mid-way point between the lowest ribcage and the iliac crest and should be measured, preferably with a special tension tape [see illustration below].

When measuring his waist, the boy should ideally be wearing only underclothes. Ask him to stand with his feet together and weight evenly distributed with his arms relaxed. Ask him to breathe normally and take the waist measurement at the end of the normal expiration.

The waist can also be identified by asking the child to bend to one side. Measurement is taken at the point of flexure.

If he is wearing a shirt or vest, deduct 1cm before recording and plotting the waist measurement.

There is no consensus about how to define paediatric obesity using waist measurement (see chart). For clinical use the 99.6th or 98th centiles are suggested cut-offs for obesity and the 91st centile for overweight, like the BMI.

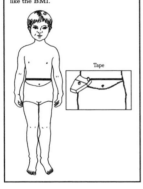

Tape

BOYS
WAIST CIRCUMFERENCE

COLE CALCULATOR TO ASSESS GROWTH/TENSION TAPE

The calculator is a pocket-sized slide rule which allows paediatric height, weight and BMI centiles/values for both genders to be easily and quickly attained. In all, the calculator may be used to attain 8 height, weight and BMI predictions and desired values for clinicians managing the treatment of patients with weight problems.

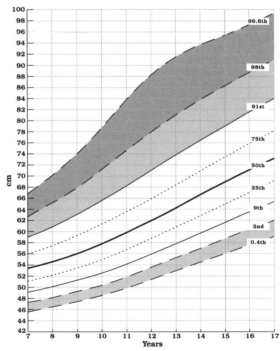

"The development of waist circumference percentiles in British children aged 5-16.9 yrs": HD McCarthy *et al: Eur J Clin Nutr* (2001): **55**: 902-907.

Because a high BMI by itself may not be a guarantor of obesity/overweight, a high waist centile added to a high BMI centile will confirm fatness more conclusively.

Measuring the waist

The waist is defined as the mid-way point between the lowest ribcage and the iliac crest and should be measured, preferably with a special tension tape [see illustration below].

When measuring her waist, the girl should ideally be wearing only underclothes. Ask her to stand with her feet together and weight evenly distributed with her arms relaxed. Ask her to breathe normally and take the waist measurement at the end of the normal expiration.

The waist can also be identified by asking the child to bend to one side. Measurement is taken at the point of flexure.

If she is wearing a shirt or vest, deduct 1cm before recording and plotting the waist measurement.

There is no consensus about how to define paediatric obesity using waist measurement (see chart). For clinical use the 99.6th or 98th centiles are suggested cut-offs for obesity and the 91st centile for overweight, like the BMI.

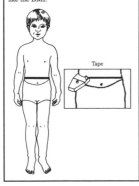

GIRLS
WAIST CIRCUMFERENCE

COLE CALCULATOR TO ASSESS GROWTH/TENSION TAPE

The calculator is a pocket-sized slide rule which allows paediatric height, weight and BMI centiles/values for both genders to be easily and quickly attained. In all, the calculator may be used to attain 8 height, weight and BMI predictions and desired values for clinicians managing the treatment of patients with weight problems.

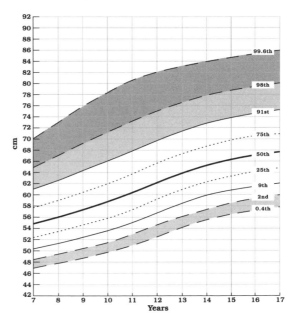

"The development of waist circumference percentiles in British children aged 5-16.9 yrs": HD McCarthy *et al: Eur J Clin Nutr* (2001): **55:** 902-907.

Referral Guidelines

BMI is used in growth monitoring to assess fatness. Although highly correlated with fatness, BMI is not a direct measure of body fat. It should therefore be interpreted with caution. Rapid changes in BMI can occur during normal childhood growth. Intervention or referral should not be based on the BMI alone.

This chart shows the standard 9 centile lines for BMI derived from UK data. The International Obesity Task Force [IOTF] has proposed paediatric cut-offs for obesity and overweight that correspond to the adult cut-offs at age 18, of BMI >30 for obesity and BMI >25 for overweight. For further information on growth and growth monitoring see:
www.heightmatters.org.uk
www.healthforallchildren.co.uk
see also these sites for the Royal College of Paediatrics & Child Health and the Natural Obesity Forum advice:
'An approach to weight management in children & adolescents [2-18yrs] in primary care'

Waist circumference is another measure of fatness and the same cautions apply. A high waist centile combined with a high BMI centile is a clearer marker of obesity than either measurement alone.

How to calculate BMI

$$BMI = \frac{weight\ [kg]}{length/height\ m^2}$$

e.g. weight=25kg height=1.2m

$$BMI = \frac{25}{1.2 \times 1.2}$$

Alternatively, use a Cole Calculator to find BMI centiles

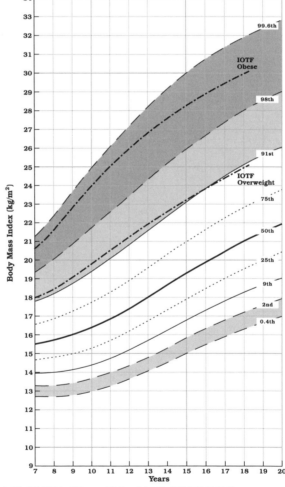

BOYS

BMI CHART

Body Mass Index reference curves for the UK, 1990 (TJ Cole, JV Freeman, MA Preece) *Arch Dis Child* 1995; **73**: 25-29
Sex differences in weight in infancy (MA Preece, JV Freeman, TJ Cole) *BMJ* 1996; **313**: 1486

Referral Guidelines

BMI is used in growth monitoring to assess fatness. Although highly correlated with fatness, BMI is not a direct measure of body fat. It should therefore be interpreted with caution. Rapid changes in BMI can occur during normal childhood growth. Intervention or referral should not be based on the BMI alone.

This chart shows the standard 9 centile lines for BMI derived from UK data. The International Obesity Task Force [IOTF] has proposed paediatric cut-offs for obesity and overweight that correspond to the adult cut-offs at age 18, of BMI >30 for obesity and BMI >25 for overweight. For further information on growth and growth monitoring see:
www.heightmatters.org.uk
www.healthforallchildren.co.uk
see also these sites for the Royal College of Paediatrics & Child Health and the Natural Obesity Forum advice:
'An approach to weight management in children & adolescents [2-18yrs] in primary care'

Waist circumference is another measure of fatness and the same cautions apply. A high waist centile combined with a high BMI centile is a clearer marker of obesity than either measurement alone.

How to calculate BMI

$$BMI = \frac{weight\ [kg]}{length/height\ m^2}$$

e.g. weight=25kg height=1.2m

$$BMI = \frac{25}{1.2 \times 1.2}$$

Alternatively, use a Cole Calculator to find BMI centiles

GIRLS
BMI CHART

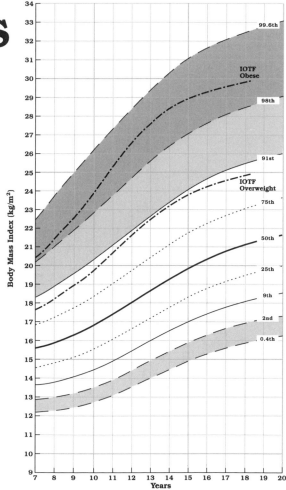

Body Mass Index reference curves for the UK, 1990 (TJ Cole, JV Freeman, MA Preece) *Arch Dis Child* 1995; **73**: 25-29
Sex differences in weight in infancy (MA Preece, JV Freeman, TJ Cole) *BMJ* 1996; **313**: 1486

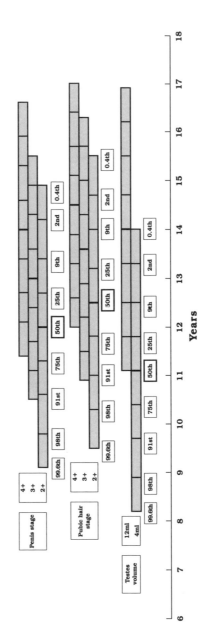

BOYS
PUBERTAL RATINGS

GIRLS
PUBERTAL RATINGS

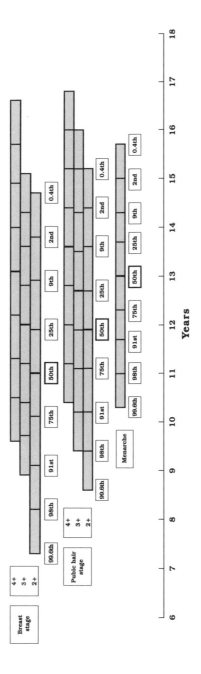

Index